AF578732

A Corpsman

Recollections of a REME Soldier
1959 – 1981

Front Cover:

Royal Electrical & Mechanical Engineer
Badge and Side hat

Kuwait Army headdress Badge pre 1962
Kuwait Army Headdress Badge post 1962

Long Service & Good Conduct Medal
(18 years service)

Rear Cover;

No 1 Trg Bn REME, Blandford,
'A' Company, No 6 Platoon (Regulars)
December 1959
The Author is sat fourth from the left on the front row.

Introduction

My alias is William Kompany
Abbreviated it becomes Bilko
And that is what people call me

Acknowledgement

I wish to thank my friend Ed Chandler, himself a published author, for his guidance and assistance in preparing this book for publication

Forward

I write this book as my recollections of my Army Career of 22 years service. Now that I am 80 years old, my memory is fading, so I apologise in advance for any errors that I may make. I recall very few names, so I have not mentioned anyone by their name, just their rank or appointment.
Some of my comments may seem strange by today's standards, but they were acceptable 40 to 60 years ago.

Contents

Chapter One.
(My childhood 1941 - 59)

My Father, a qualified Electrician, came from a family of five children. His Mother was continually Ill, so both his education and life as the oldest son were affected, as he had the responsibility of caring for his younger siblings. At sixteen he left Secondary School and obtained an Apprenticeship with a firm of Electricians, this became his main career. His hobbies were carpentry, decorating, and he was a very good Handyman at most things.

My Mother was educated in a Grammar School, and she was competent in English, French and Mathematics. As a progression from the Grammar School she went onto further education in one of the Pitman Colleges of Secretarial training, she sort employment as a Comptometer Operator, best described as a mathematical calculator, with the aid of an adding machine, the fore runner to the electronic calculator. Her hobbies were cross word puzzles, the football pools and knitting.

Myself, I was educated up to Junior School, but failed the eleven plus exam, so I was directed to Secondary School. But, my Mother had other ideas, my parents decided to send me to a Private College, in Ilford, Essex, for which they had to pay for everything. I believe this College was linked to the Pitman Group of Colleges. There was continual Homework, which affected my

social life and freedom with my neighbour's children. A 'Snob' was the term of the day. I wanted to join the Metropolitan Police College at the age of sixteen, but I failed the entrance exam, reasons unknown. My next choice of career was the Merchant Navy, but, again I failed the entrance exam, but this time on medical grounds, I was colour blind. My third choice of career was as a Psychiatric Nurse, the examination was with a Psychiatrist, who recommended that I return to education to gain my General Certicates of Education (GCE's) required for Nursing. So I enrolled in a Technical College in Barking, Essex in 1958. After one year of the two year course I went on holiday as a student to Corsica with the College Group.
On return to the UK I developed septic feet, because I had come into contact with Sea Urchins in Corsica, and needed urgent treatment, resulting in the removal of my big toe nails. Because of this I missed the return to College for the 1959 Autumn Term, and consequently lost my place and education. I was now just eighteen years old and available for Conscription (National Service) into the Forces. So I made the quick decision, that it was better and more advantageous, to enlist as a Regular Soldier.

In 1939 the National Service Act was implemented by the Government, this covered all Services including Police, Fire, Coalminers, Railwaymen etc, in addition to the Army, Navy and Royal Air Force. Anyone engaged under this Act was classed as Conscripted. So, if you were 'Called Up' you were 'Conscripted' in addition to the Regular Forces, this was commonly known as National Service.

Chapter Two:
(The British Army 1959)

In 1959, the British Army along with the Royal Navy and the Royal Air Force were controlled by the War Office, and Conscription was still a requirement for all available eighteen year old men until it's cessation in 1961.

Back then the constitution of the Army was a multiple of Regiments and Corps. Regiments were basically Infantry or other Military skills. Corps consisted of Soldiers with a variety of Trade Skills. We were all taught basic Military Training, but then continued to be employed as Tradesmen, always a Soldier, but with a Trade Skill. In these roles we supported various Units, as Mechanics, Electricians, Welders, Aircraft and Radar Technicians, also Marine Engineers etc.

In smaller units the Workshop was called a Light Aid Detachment (LAD), carrying out minor to medium repairs, basically maintenance. There were also Regimental Workshops, that performed medium repairs and maintenance.

The Corps of the Royal Electrical & Mechanical Engineers (REME) also had its own Independent Workshops, usually a Command Workshop, medium to major repairs, or a Base Workshop (being the biggest), carryout out major overhauls or rebuilds.

The Army was located not just in the UK, but in various strategic locations around the world, West German, Aden, Singapore and Hong Kong for example. In each of these locations would usually be a Command Workshop, plus all the Units and their respective LADs. At its peak, the REME as a Corps reached over 40,000 men, the biggest single element (Corps) in the British Army.

Chapter Three
(My Enlistment & Training 1959 - 61)

To enlist I had to go to the Recruiting Office in Walthamstow, London. The procedure there was to be given a small written aptitude test to highlight your current abilities and interests. My test showed that I was a keen model maker, interested in electric motors and electricity. I had already decided that I wanted to join the REME, but my trade was yet to be decided. On the recommendations of the Recruiting Sergeant, it was suggested that I should go for one of the Electronic Trades.

My length of service was the next question? In those days you could commit for a 22 year contract, with options of stages of three years i.e.: 3, 6 or 9 years (being the longest then available), the greater number of years that you chose received a higher pay scale. By comparison, Conscripts were receiving less than £3 per week; my pay was to start at about £5 per week. On completion of Trade Training this rose to around £6, another reason for me to volunteer.

So I enlisted for a 22years with the 9 year option, and into an Electronic trade, which again was the highest paid. After taking the Oath of Allegiance and signing the necessary paperwork I returned home to await my Call Up papers. My papers duly arrived a few days later and I was ordered to report to Number One Training Battalion at Blandford Forum in Somerset. No 1 Trg Bn

REME was a basic Military skills training unit, also used by Conscripts. I am glad that I had made the right decision to volunteer because on a daily basis we could see the rough treatment that Conscripts had to undergo.
From the very beginning I found it difficult to 'fit in' with the other recruits because of my education and 'posh' accent, so I tried to down tone my speech and was finally accepted. My popularity soon increased when my room mates realized that I could iron, sew, 'bull' boots and polish brasses.

On the first day we were issued with all our uniforms, equipment and bedding, then told to pack up our civilian clothes and we were given brown paper and string to send them to our families. You're in the Army now!
We received Fatigue Dress, which consisted of Denim Trousers and a blouson jacket. Our main uniform was the woollen Battledress trousers and blouson jacket, as worn from the end of the Second World War. Boots were Ammunition Boots, hard, stiff and uncomfortable until worn in, many blisters were gained in the meantime. These boots had metal heel and toe plates, with studs on the soles, which we had to fit, and when first worn, were extremely slippery on smooth surfaces until we got used to them.

Webbing was the post war pattern, Web belt; two cross shoulder straps, with two ammunition pouches worn on the front. On our backs we wore a large pack and a small pack. Hung from the side of our belts was the metal water bottle with wool covering. Also issued was a kitbag, small bayonet scabbard to be worn on the belt and web gaiters for our trouser bottoms. All buckles and fastenings were brass. Not forgetting a steel helmet, under which we could wear a strange tubular woollen sleeve called a cap comforter, it also doubled up as a scarf. With the battledress (BD) we wore a greatcoat of wool, and woollen gloves in cold weather.

Other items included a small rolled pouch which contained needles, thread and a length of wool, called a housewife, a pocket knife with folding blades, a pair of boot brushes and mess tins with a knife, fork, spoon and a china mug completed the collection. Over all this we were expected to wear a large waterproof sheet called a groundsheet in inclement weather.

All this equipment we were expected to clean, press, polish and blanco to military standards. It was a sharp learning curve. Resulting in countless inspections, almost on a daily basis, anything not up to standard was either thrown across the barrack floor or out of the nearest open window, usually accompanied with a rain of verbal abuse from the examiner, anyone from a Lance Corporal to the Sergeant Major. Our accommodation at Blandford was the old wooden spider formations, a central toilet and wash room unit from which six separate dormitories projected, hence the name spider. Each dormitory accommodated about 14 soldiers, with a small room just inside the entrance for our Training NCO.

The dormitory had to be cleaned and polished daily, windows gleaming, and the wooden flooring waxed and buffered to a high sheen, and woe betide anyone who walked on it with studded boots.

Training consisted of endless square bashing until we could all move in unison in the same direction. Other foot drills were also taught, field craft, hygiene and the composition of the Army. Shooting on the ranges was a new skill to most of us, and a basic standard had to be achieved here as well. Physical training was also to be endured with countless PT lessons, assault course antics and routine marches as a squad which seemed to never end, especially in cold and inclement weather.

An example of a Drill lesson went as follows:

"Get them knees up!" Shouted the Sergeant, whilst trying to give the timing "One, Tup – One Tup".
"Get yur dressing" "One Tup – One Tup"
"Get in line, One Tup – One Tup".
"On the spot, On the spot, Don't wanda orf".
So this is what the army is all about? I thought to myself. Marching to stay on the spot, doesn't make much sense.
"Get them thighs level to the ground, knees up!" continued the Sergeant.
My thoughts wondered, why can't we just stand still? It would be a lot easier –
"Your not paying attention laddie" shouted the Sergeant in my ear. Now get back in line and get them knees up!".
Phoo! This is getting tedious, I began to think to myself, as I'm beginning to tire, my legs are aching because I'm not being used to all this exercise.
"Your not trying laddie" shouted the Sergeant at someone else, much to my relief.
"One – Tup, One – Tup".

"Get them boots higher" came the instruction.
I know where I'd like to stick my boot thought I to myself, and who I'd like to do it to.
"Keep your dressing" "One – Tup – One Tup"
He can't even speak properly, thought I again.
I suddenly felt a knee hit me in my buttocks accompanied by those words of wisdom
"Keep your dressing laddie"
My legs were beginning to feel like they were lead, up - down, left – right, left –right, again and again. I was beginning to wish I hadn't eaten all that egg and bacon for my breakfast, I could feel it swishing about inside me. Not surprising, considering it's getting all this jerking about.
"Are you getting tired laddie?" asked the Sergeant in my ear.
"No Sergeant" was my breathless reply, not trying to show my fatigue.
"Good laddie, then let's have more effort"
Effort? Effort? – I am flagging from effort. Doesn't he know when to stop? The energy was slowly draining from me, and I could hear the laboured heavy breathing of others in the squad. I thought will this never stop?
I could feel my new boots rubbing the skin on my feet. Up – down, up – down, feeling sorer at each contact with the ground.
THEN, came THE command -
"Squad – Alt!"
Such joyous words.
Now we were trying to stand still, because our legs were like jelly and wouldn't stop moving.
"Don't you want to make your father's proud of you?" sniped the Sergeant.

The unanimous silent response from the squad was “Bet he doesn’t know who his father was? B*****d !”

The only relief that we had, if we had the time, was the NAAFI or the Salvation Army canteen, because during basic training we were all confined to camp. There were several new squads training at the same time, including Conscripts, so inter squad rivalry was always evident. But after six weeks of this initiation and pain, came the passing out parade, at which the best squad was announced. This time our squad was the lucky one. During this period my operated feet began to flare up, because of the toe capped boots, and they often bled, needing Medical attention.

One thing I did enjoy during training, was firing various weapons on the ranges, I even managed to qualify as a Marksman on the Lee Enfield .303 rifle and the Bren Gun (LMG).

Basic Military Training over, I was now given the rank of Private (Pte), and we were all posted to our respective Trade Training units, mine was to be No 3 Training Battalion at Arborfield, Berkshire where I arrived in early 1960.

Until there were sufficient students to compose a Course we were employed on general duties, basically doing any dirty jobs within the camp that nobody else wanted to do. After a couple of weeks our Trade Training Course started. The first weeks were basic electric circuitry and constructing wiring looms around and over objects. Next came the introduction to resistors, a small cylindrical component with different colour markings upon it to denote its value or purpose. Each of us was given a peg board into which we plugged our components as we constructed various circuits. For me this was where the fun started, because following verbal or written instructions, I composed my circuits, or so I thought, and then when we switched our circuits 'on', mine invariably went Phut! with an accompanying 'bang and a puff of smoke'. Initially this confused my Instructors, but then they discovered I was colour blind, and so ended my hopes of being an Electronic Technician.

Previously, on Enlistment at the Recruiting Office I had to state three choices of trade in order of preference. I listed Electronic Technician, Vehicle Mechanic and last of all an Electrician. My electronic training now gone up in smoke, I was relocated to Vehicle Mechanic training.
In early summer I arrived at No 8 Training Battalion, Norton Manor camp near Taunton, Somerset. I was allocated to Wheeled Vehicle (B) training, the others being Armoured Vehicles (A) or Construction equipment (C).

As the course progressed we learnt about chassis, transmission, steering, brakes, carburetion and a variety of engine types. The course was interesting, especially the diesel part of it. Ironically we were introduced to basis vehicle wiring, but I didn't have a problem here as it was only two wires, red and black.

During the course we had a lot more freedom and could wear civilian clothes and own vehicles. My choice was a motor cycle that I had just purchased and so used it to travel to and from the camp. It was parked on an allocated car park within the camp.

It was whilst I was on Guard duty at the armoury at the far end of the camp one night that I recognised the sound of my motor bike. On completion of my shift I returned to the Guard Room to discovery that my bike had been recorded in the Booking Out Register, so I mentioned it to the Guard Commander, who on return to the camp, the rider was arrested and placed in one of the cells. I moved my bike back to the park, but noticed that it had been damaged in an accident. Next morning the rider appeared before the Commanding Officer and was given 28 days detention in the unit Guard Room.

The rider was from 'A' Company and I was in 'B' Company, and it happened that the rider's mates had decided to retaliate, by cutting through my rubber fuel pipe between the fuel tank and carburettor. The result was that the next time I rode the bike, fuel was leaking onto the engine and I quickly ran out of fuel and was stranded in the middle of nowhere. I pushed the bike to a Garage, left a note and returned to camp. This was my first experience of 'military comradeship and barrack justice'.

Having completed the Vehicle Mechanic Course, I was give the rank of Craftsman (Cfn) and classed as a Group 'A' Tradesman (for pay scale rates) and I was awarded the trade qualification of being 'B' vehicle trained, albeit at Class 3 level. Then to our surprise we were allocated to another period of vehicle training. This time it was the additional qualification of Vehicle Electricians (E). Finally finishing all this training I was awarded the trade qualification of 'BE Class 3', vehicle and electrician trained.

During my course, one day in October 1960, I went on my motorbike to Yeovil to visit the camp there, which was a mixture of male and females also in training. It was here that I met my future wife in the NAAFI that evening. There followed a courtship with many journeys between Taunton and Yeovil when the opportunities arose, by early 1961 we became engaged.

In addition to my vehicle training my Records Office sent me to the School of Electrical & Mechanical Engineers (SEME) at Bordon, Hampshire, to attend yet another course, this time it was Light Armoured Vehicles.

Another four to six weeks of introduction into the world of automatic epicyclic gearboxes, hydraulics, and gear reduction hubs with torsion bar suspension. Whoopee!
Having now been further educated I was granted the Specialist Qualification of 'Armoured Car Trained'. Now came the hard bit, to be able to use all this information in a working unit.

This course completed I was sent to the Corps Depot at Arborfield, for onward posting to my first working unit.

Chapter Four
South Arabia 1961 – 63

Having reported to Depot REME I was placed on General Duties until the decision had been reached as to where I should be posted. It was whilst I was waiting for posting I went before my Company Commander at the Depot to ask permission to get married. Queen's Regulations of the time required that if I intended to get married, I had to ask the permission of my Company Commander, especially as I was then only 19 years old. Permission was granted, so my Wife and I were married in Aberdeen (her home town). a month later. In the meantime we both returned to Scotland on leave to make all the arrangements.

The week prior to our marriage I visited my parents in London on the Tuesday evening, on my way to Scotland, and told them we were getting married the following Saturday. We had already had The Banns declared on our previous trip to Aberdeen, and as the marriage was to be in Scotland my parents could not prevent it. The marriage was a small affair with just our close family members in attendance.

When the Notification of postings came through, I was to be sent to Aden Workshop. First question was "Where the heck is Aden?".

On discovering where Aden was, it was at least a foreign post in a warm climate. I was then issued with my tropical climate uniform, and waited to move.
My wife by then had returned to her Unit and under Queen's Regulation was granted her discharge from the Service upon which she returned to Aberdeen to stay with her father. At the end of June the Movement Orders finally came through, and I was to embark at Southampton and travel to Aden by sea.

Having said my farewells to my Wife and parents my journey started on a Troop Train to Southampton. As the Train drew to a halt on the quayside at Southampton Docks, we all knew that we were setting off from the shores of England to foreign lands in the call of duty as Servicemen. It was now late June 1961 and National Service was still in force, so along with Regulars, around 750 in all, we all embarked upon the Troopship SS Nevasa for idyllic named locations all the way to Hong Kong, Families had gathered on the quayside to wave goodbye, and there was many a tearful eye on land and ship, the atmosphere was a little sullen. By mid afternoon we were all aboard, and the ship's crew prepared to set sail.

Having stowed all our kit away in the decks below, we all returned to the ship's rails to make our last farewells. The ship eased away from the quay and out into the sounds, gradually gaining speed. It was tea time so the majority of us went to the ship's galley for our meal, but once over, some of us returned to the ship's rails to get a last glimpse of home as it faded into the sunset.

The first evening we were all kept busy with making ourselves familiar with the ship's routine and getting our kit sorted for the journey ahead. Sleeping in dormitories of bunks three high, was not easy, and the noise level never seemed to drop, even during the night with all the snoring and other sounds.

Being in a ship is like being inside a tin can, the slightest noise at one end reverberates right through the vessel, add to this the unrelenting motion of the sea, and there were many who regretted eating any food at all, and could only see green. Sailing from the English Channel and entering the Bay of Biscay, was too much for us landlubbers, and there were many dizzy heads and disturbed stomachs, and nobody had any sea legs. But as the journey progressed we gradually became accustomed to it and managed to stay upright.

Single and unaccompanied Servicemen were accommodated below decks, but families were accommodated elsewhere in cabins, and with there being children on board as well, we were given daily duties of manning the ship's rails to safeguard the families.

Leaving the Bay of Biscay and entering the short length of the Atlantic before reaching Gibraltar was the worst part of the sailing and we were all glad when 'The Rock' appeared, and we sailed past it into the calmer waters of the Mediterranean.

Nor did the ship have to stop at Malta either, so we sailed onward in the warm sunlight and calmer sea reaching the entrance to the Suez Canal, where the ship had to anchor at Port Said in order to let ships travelling north clear the canal before we could travel south. Anchored directly opposite the Nevasa was the P&O Ship SS Oriana, full of tourists and passengers travelling to Europe. Again it was tea time, and after our meal with nothing else to do we all came up on deck into the cooler evening air. On board the Oriana the passengers were having a dinner and dance, as we could hear the sounds of the ship's orchestra drifting across the water, and passengers in dinner dress were stood out on the decks waving to us because their ship's Captain had already announced that we were a Troopship heading for the Far East.

As if by magic, musical instruments began appearing on the Nevasa's deck, and led by some bagpipes, our musicians began to play and we started to sing in accompaniment, about 400 of us. To our amazement, more passengers on the Oriana appeared at the ship's rails, and we continued playing and singing. The Oriana's orchestra eventually stopped playing, and all that could be heard in Port Said was our music continuing until after the sun had set behind the Oriana and it was too dark for us to stay on deck. We then retired to our bunks.

Early next morning the Nevasa had moved nearer towards the entrance of the canal proper, and where the channel narrowed there appeared the Arab Traders in their ramshackle boats, or 'bum boats' as we called them – each boat laden with goods of eastern promise.

Bartering began with some of the Arabs, and a weight was thrown up to the ship's deck with a string attached to it, followed by the instruction from the Arab to place the money into the basket tied to the string. As the basket was being lowered back to the Arab the Soldier changed his mind, and tried to pull the basket with his money back upwards. There followed a brief tug-o-war between the Soldier and the Arab. The string broke, and the basket with its contents fell into the Arab's boat, much to the annoyance of the Soldier. As we had been returning from breakfast we each had our china mugs with us, so the dissatisfied Soldier leaned over the ship's rail and let his mug drop towards the Arab's boat, which it hit and 'exploded' by the Arab. Shouts went out from both the Arabs and the Soldiers, and chaos was created, with numerous missiles showering down upon the Arabs. Shrill whistles were heard as the Military Police on board started to try to apprehend the offenders. The ship's crew were instructed to turn on the fire hoses and aim them at the Arabs in order to make them withdraw. But secretly, another barter was taking place from one of the lower portholes, where ship's blankets were being passed to a delighted Arab. In a matter of moments the decks had been cleared and the Arabs were out of range of the water, but, it was entertaining whilst it had lasted. The ship moved into the canal and left the Arabs behind.

Of the Suez Canal there was little to be seen, just high sand banking with the occasional villagers doing their washing in the canal waters, palm trees, camels, and children waving to us were the only other sights of interest.

Leaving the canal behind the ship picked up speed again in the Red Sea, where the heat was becoming unbearable during the day, the ship's decks became too hot and there was little breeze. All the port holes and gangways were open, it was like an oven and we were allowed to go up on deck at night to sleep. We used to while away the hours watching the dolphins and other fish leaping out of the water and racing with the ship. Approaching the Horn of Africa on our right, Aden was on our left and during the night the Nevasa dropped anchor in the sheltered harbour, and early next morning, those who were posted to Aden disembarked into the motor launches and were taken to the quayside. It may have only been early in the day but we were all soaking wet with perspiration due to the high humidity.

On the quayside we waited to be transported to our respective units to report for duty, whilst the Nevasa continued on her journey further east. It was then we all felt a lump in our throats as we watched her sailing away, leaving us stranded here, and victims of the heat and smells of Arabia. The reality now hit each of us as we stood there, just how far we had travelled, and we each silently felt a long way from home.

Aden is a Port at the very southern extremity of Saudi Arabia and is basically a deep sea harbour formed by an extinct volcano on the south side, with an isthmus on the east side joining it to the mainland on the north side. It had been a refuelling station, first coal now oil fuel, for ships travelling to and from the Far East, and Australia for over 100 years, and was in 1961 still a British Protectorate. The Port of Aden was also a Custom's

Duty Free Port, which made it very popular with tourist ships as they travelled by.

The volcano called Shamsan, was large enough to accommodate the Crater City, but on the outer northern slopes were the areas of Tawahi (Steamer Point to us), Maalla (an area of flats and Arab houses with a few shops.) stretching west to the flat sandy area of the Military Units turning north onto the isthmus to Khormasar where the Royal Air Force had its Airfield and family accommodations. At the top of the isthmus was the Arab village of Sheik Othman, after which the population thinned very quickly into desert land.

Most tourist visitors confined themselves to the 'bargain' shops of Steamer Point. Between 1961 and 1963 was a relative 'quiet period' politically in Aden, albeit there were some incidents and skirmishes, but not on the scale of later years when the British prepared to relinquish the territory to Arab control, finally in 1967.
There were areas where we ordered not to go, the areas of most Arab concentration, Crater City back streets and the village of Sheik Othman.

The back streets of Steamer Point could also be dangerous at times. The straight of Maalla had to be treated with caution. As a short cut between the south and north shores of the harbour, and bypassing Sheik Othman, there was a bridged road called the Causeway, which the Services used in preference to passing the Khormaksar and Sheik Othman areas.

The causeway led to a road running east to west along the northern shore of the harbour. At the eastern end was Sheik Othman, in the middle was located the barracks of the Local Military Force, the Aden Proctectorate Levies, but on the western end was the area known as Little Aden.

Little Aden was where the BP fuel refining and fuelling station was, with some civilian and military accommodation and a unit of Royal Marines was also based there.

Continuing northward from Little Aden through the low hills of 'Silent Valley' after a couple of miles you come onto the flat expanse of the start of the desert which reaches miles to the far north and the foothills of the then Yemen. But, tucked away just north of the low hills near Silent Valley, is an area called Falaise, where there was another Army camp consisting of Royal Engineers and the Army Air Corps, who's airstrip and Workshops were located just over a mile further north on the beginning of the desert.

A majority of Units and Workshops and Stores Depots were located on the area between Khormaksar and the Crater, on the eastern side of the harbour. It was here at Singapore Lines where Aden Workshop and it's accommodation was located, my new home and place of work.

The Workshop consisted of a number of large hangars and smaller buildings to facilitate all the various trades and working areas.

The accommodation was long prefabricated single storey buildings with rooms for single or four men rooms, in the centre of each block was the ablution area. Each building had a veranda, in front of which was just a sandy gap between each building block.

Each morning we would all parade for roll call then march to the Workshop to start work about 0700hrs, and we worked until noon, when the heat became unbearable and we returned to our accommodaton to clean up and change.

As I was Armoured Car trained I was employed in that Section of the Workshop. My particular daily task was removing, stripping and re-building suspension units. This entailed removing damaged or worn parts, reassembling with new components, and then recalibrating each unit before refitting them back onto the vehicle. Part of the refit was to reconnect the hydraulic braking system, which after 'bleeding' free of air had to be tested. The best way to do this was to carryout a Road Test, which also was an excuse to get out of the Workshop for a drive.

Unfortunately Armoured vehicles have very limited driver's view capabilities, and it was necessary to have a passenger 'up top' in the turret for safety. As my work had to be 'cleared' by a Senior NCO Examiner, he could 'double up' as the passenger.

So it was that I set off out of the Workshop in the Armoured Car, with my scrutinising passenger in

position. We didn't have any headsets to be able to use the intercom, so all communication was by shouting at each other over the sound of the vehicle.
The approved Brake Test Route was a tarmac road along the coastline, where the beach came right up to the road itself, with nothing but sand on either side of the road.
I was given the instruction by the NCO that when he 'banged' on the hatch that I was to brake, to test the efficiency of my work.

I set off down the tarmac gradually building up my speed, just short of 30 mph I heard a bang, and so as instructed, I braked. Next second, to my surprise, I saw out of the corner of my right eye an Arab Mercedes Taxi come skidding past me in a cloud of loose sand. The driver obviously having trouble trying to control his vehicle, which eventually came to a juddering halt in a pile of sand, much to the shaken driver's relief.

My vehicle also came to a halt, but the NCO was shouting down to me "What did I think I was doing? He added that I had very nearly had a speeding Mercedes impaled on my rear end.

I told him that I had heard a 'bang' and had braked as instructed. He then enlightened me that I had gone over a hole in the tarmac which had made the loose hatch cover 'jump' and bang. Later we both laughed at the narrow miss. My work passed the inspection.

In the evening our main recreation used to be watching films hired from the SKC (Services Kinema Corporation). Our Cinema was in the open between the billet blocks. Initially the screen was a canvas one on a frame, tied to the side of a truck. Our seats were our chairs from the accommodation, the projector stood on a table.

Watching films from home was our way of escaping our rather bland surroundings. That was until one night the film was 'Ice Cold in Alex' starring John Mills. This particular evening it was a bit chilly, so the audience sat huddled in blankets.

As the film progressed, it came to the sand storm scene. Engrossed in the story we sat glued to the screen, unaware that the wind was howling and the sand was blowing around us as well. So engrossed was the audience that we failed to notice that we too were sat in a sand storm, but no-one moved from their seat. Like the actors we stuck it to the end.

No special effects, the realism of the storm only added to the thrill of the film.

I took an interest in being the Projectionist, and it evolved that I was sent to the Services Kinema Corporation Cinema (SKC) at Khormaksar for training, and so I acquired an additional qualification of Projectionist in both 16 & 35mm projection.

Aden being a Duty Free Port meant minimum tax on all goods bought, and it was an opportunity to buy cameras in particular, at very reasonable prices. Having made friends with an Arab shop owner, being a frequent visitor to him, and knowing that if he did not stock a particular request, he would dispatch his boy runner to bring the item from another shop owner, a very convenient way for me to buy things, then we would settle down to 'barter' the price.

To an Arab bartering is a source of entertainment and necessity, it could take a long time over many glasses of Chia (Arab tea), or bottles of Cola. But usually ends with both parties being satisfied. It is worth mentioning that if an Arab gives a price, and the buyer accepts it straight away, the Arab is disappointed, because he regrets not asking more money for the item in the first place. Conversely, if the buyer barters for the lowest price he can get from the seller, the Arab is satisfied that he has obtained from the buyer as much money as the buyer is prepared to offer. Many a happy hour was spent in this fashion, and led to me purchasing many items from this Arab, to his delight. I did purchase a Yashica 635 Twin Lens Reflex Camera (the poor man's equivalent of the more expensive Rolaflex), and with this camera I started to photograph views of Aden and it's events.

As part of the recreation policy of the Workshop, it supplied a fully equipped Dark Room, which I quickly started to use. Photos were originally for my own use, but as time went by I started to produce and sell them to other soldiers, even taking portraits to be sent home, and it became a little 'side line' that provided funds for me to purchase other and better camera equipment.

One of the Workshop's Military Duties was to provide mechanics to accompany the fortnightly resupply

convoys to Dhala, an Up Country Post near the Yemen border.
The day began at 0300hrs reveille, followed by breakfast and collection of a day's food rations, next to the armoury to collect a personal weapon and 50 rounds of ammunition. With my mechanic's toolbox I joined my transport, a Bedford 3 tonner with a canvas canopy where the side panels had been removed, only the top canvas remained for shade.

The convoy assembly point was along the beach road near to Khormaksar, and we set off just before dawn, speeding through the outskirts of Sheik Othman northwards towards the banana plantation.

The convoy consisted of over twenty vehicles, cargo trucks carrying the necessary supplies, food, water and ammunition etc, there were trucks carrying platoons of infantry, and small armoured vehicles, Ferrets, for protection. The road was dusty and dry, and because our vehicle was in the latter part of the convoy, we suffered from all the dust, having to half cover our faces with clothe and our eyes with goggles.

As the sun rose, so did the heat, there was little fresh air, it was all dust.

Having moved from the most populated areas, the convoy quickly passed through a series of smaller villages until we were in open country, with little to be seen, and the ground got rougher. For a period the convoy drove along a dried river bed, a Whadi, until we drove up and onto a plateau island where the Whadi had split into two rivers, forming this plateau. Here we stopped for a short rest, with nothing in sight. But within minutes children began to appear, and they started begging for anything we were prepared to give them, it was a pityful sight, but we had to keep them away from the vehicles.

We continued the journey north, towards the foothills of the Yemen border. Our next stop period was at an Arab Fort in the foot hills, here supplies were offloaded for the local force and the British Contingent.

The foot hills were fast approaching, getting taller and the track was getting narrower, and we had entered into shrub land as well, with the occasional tree but with lots of tall grasses. It was here that one of the landrovers broke down and I had to help to repair it. I remember being nervous and aware of my surroundings because we had an armoured car stop by us to provide protective fire if we needed it, as we were now overlooked by foot hills, from where Arabs were known to take ‘pot shots’ at the convoys. An Officer and his driver had been killed in an incident not many months before.

Having repaired the landrover we continued to follow the convoy, the driving was now getting harder as the track began to rise higher on the side of the rocky valley that we were in. The vehicles at the front of the convoy could be seen in the distance a lot higher up the track and above us. The progress was slow, and very narrow, with lots of winding bends. At one bend, it was an hair bend, where all the vehicles could only drive forward so far, and then had to reverse, before moving forward again to complete the turn. Here we dismounted from the truck, for safety sake, because some trucks in convoys past had not manoeuvred this bend safely and had ended up in the valley bottom a long way below. Any vehicle that broke down on this part of the journey and could not be repaired, was unloaded, and ended up with the same fate as those at the valley bottom.

This part of the journey we were all on our guard as it was a very vulnerable part of the trip. Having reached the top of the track, the convoy drove into a wide open valley with small hills. It was on one of these low hills that the Army Base of Dhala was encamped.

Encamped is literally the word, it was a tented village surrounded by protective walls and gun emplacements. The convoy drove into the camp and all the supplies were rapidly offloaded, along with welcomed mail from home. It was now late afternoon, and too late to return to Aden, so we were given temporary accommodation for the night. We were only too glad to use the hose pipe shower facilities to wash off the day's grime.

And having eaten nothing but dried sandwiches for the day were looking forward to a proper cooked meal. Here, we were given a 'lesson' in upcountry eating.

The Cook's kitchen and serving area was one large tent, and the dinning area was another large tent, both tents were about 15 yards apart, and it was here that the 'dash' began. Those who had chosen to not 'heed' to advice given, did come a cropper. The more seasoned upcountry soldier had learnt how to have his meal served in the kitchen tent. We had all been issued with our pair of mess tins, and china mugs. With these we were expected to collect our main meal, invariably a form of stew with vegetables in one tin, into the other tin would go our pudding, usually a form of pie with custard. Additional to this we would each collect at least a couple of slices of bread, and a full mug of bromide tea. Those in the know, would carry all this in one hand, with the free hand left to protect it. Because a local flock of Kite hawks had taken a liking to army cooking, and would swoop on the unenlighted soldier as he tried to run the 15 yards between the two tents with his meal. The birds would swoop with the speed and accuracy of dive bombers snatching anything the soldier was carrying that had not been protected. This led to much entertainment and laughter amongst the soldiers who had managed to enter the dinning tent unmolested.

Those who had been victims, either embarrassingly eat what was left, or sheepishly returned to the smiling Cooks to beg for more. These Kite hawks had been renamed by the soldiers with a similar sounding name, but with a soldier's twist.

We later retired to our sleeping accommodation for the night. Reveille was again early in the morning, but just as dawn was breaking. We needed the daylight to descend the tracked pass. Again, we stopped for a pause at the Arab Fort and again on the plateau, after which it was an uneventful journey back to the dispersal point and return to our respective units.

I would like to take the opportunity here to mention three local Arabs whom I shall always remember.

The first was a Coach Trimmer who worked in the REME Workshop. Each morning and at the cessation of work he could be heard moving down the tarmac road, because of the way that he 'walked'. Apparently, when he was a child his family had tied both his legs up behind his back, so that he could become a Beggar (then a considered honourable profession). As he grew older his legs withered, and he used leather straps to tie them to the back of his waistband. This meant that he could only move about on his hands and knees. Now that he was grown up, he used wooden blocks to walk on, one pair on his knees and the other pair held in his hands, this enabled him to move on all fours. Not wishing to sound unkind, but when he 'walked' in this fashion he sounded like a small pony trotting.

The second Arab was only a very small man and frail by our standards, but he used to drive the Workshop Mobile Crane around the compound carrying out various tasks. The Crane was an old Coles Crane with an upright steering column, but because of his small stature, the operating peddles had to be fitted with wooden blocks, so that his feet could reach them to enable him to drive it. He also used to drive a cut-down landrover with a small crane on the rear. To help make him proficient at driving both vehicles he had been taught by wearing a pair of old shoes which were painted different colours to correspond with the various peddles.

The third Arab was a conman with only one arm. He used to stand at the roundabout outside the Camp gates, where he used to accost servicemen on their way out of the various camps. His usual method of operation was that he would try to obtain money from unsuspecting soldiers, by offering them a variety of goods or services. He would promise to fetch anything for them, but only if he was given five East African Shillings in advance. Some soldiers fell for the ruse and they could be observed stood waiting for the Arab's return – which he never did, not that day anyway. He became known as the original One Armed Bandit.

Our mid morning 'break' was another source of amusement. As soon as the Workshop Bell rang there was a mad rush to get to the Somalia hut to buy a roll filled with tomato, onion, and a bottle of Stim or Sinalco (local fizzy drinks). No matter how quick we soldiers were, we never got to the Hut before at least a dozen Arabs. There always ensued arguments and hassling for us to buy our snacks, but we soon learnt that the Arabs have a dislike of some of our habits, one of which was for some of the soldiers to take a small still stick with which they 'tickled' the rear of any Arab in front of them in the queue. These Arabs reacted with indignity shouting "Abe, abe, mavish abe" (shame, shame, have you no shame?), at the same time the Arab would take hold of the tuft of his beard and jump out of the queue - One pace forward for the soldiers.

Within three months of arriving in Aden, I was told to pack up my kit and be ready to move next morning. I was also instructed to collect my personal rifle and to be sure that I wore civilian clothes and I was given my passport. Unofficially the word went round the billets that night that there was a 'flap' on and that a group of us were to being moved to Bahrain.

Next morning at the appointed time we all paraded by the transport that was to take us to the RAF airfield at Khormaksar. Looking around we all realised that we were of mixed trades skills, mechanics, vehicle electricians, armoured car specialists and a few tank mechanics, about twenty of us altogether.

At the airfield our rifles were taken from us and placed in a crate, marked 'Vehicle Parts', and our kitbags were stowed in an awaiting aircraft, a Hastings, into which we filed and secured ourselves in the seats provided.

The flight to Bahrain was long and tedious, as the aircraft was only a two engine craft and it vibrated like mad. The views from the windows were limited and monotonous - undulating hills of sand.

Arriving at Bahrain we were transported to the tented lines of the Parachute Regiment where we were told to stay out of the way until our documentation and arrangements had been completed for the next part of our journey. Again, the whisper went round that we were heading for Kuwait. Nobody knew anything of it.
Leaving Bahrain a few days later we boarded a civil aircraft that did fly to Kuwait, however, we did not land at the civil airport but at a newly constructed airport that had not yet been commissioned. There were only Kuwait army personnel waiting to greet us, and they

were guarding the airport. Boarding a Kuwait Army bus we were driven off along the coast road with nothing to view but sand and sea.

Our accommodation turned out to be part of the Kuwait Oil Company, a group of bungalow buildings in a fenced compound adjacent to the refinery at the edge of the sea, at Minah el Ahmedi. Apart from the English caretaker and his wife we were the only occupants.

Later we gathered in the mess hall, and for the first time were told why we were there. Our purpose was to maintain a group of vehicles and equipment that the British Army had 'secreted' there, with the agreement of the Kuwait Government, to be held in a state of readiness for any eventuality. Apparently, in 1960 there had been a threatened invasion of Kuwait by Iraq, and in order to preserve the oilfields and the newly declared independence of Kuwait from British Rule, the Sheik had requested unofficial British support – Us - We formed the nucleus of what was to become The Kuwait Liaison Team. For all intense and purposes the British Army had loaned us to the Kuwait Army, we were clothed in Kuwaiti uniforms, fed and accommodated by the Kuwait Army, we wore the Kuwait Army headdress and cap badge, and to our delight we were paid by Kuwait. Again, we were told not to draw attention to ourselves, but we were allowed to go to the nearby oil town that was managed by the English Oil Company. It was like an oasis in the desert, with all the facilities of a Surrey Country Club, even a golf course.

Our daily transport to work was a bus of the variety seen in American programmes as a school bus, the only difference was that our bus was not yellow, but painted desert sand. We used to take it in turns to drive the bus ourselves each day.

We boarded the bus at our billets near the Oil Rfinery and travelled towards Kuwait City before turning off the coast road in the direction of our destination, an unused Sheik's palace.

We had two choices of travel, one to take the road all the way there, or, one which we favoured most days was to turn off the coast road early into the desert and follow a row of telegraph poles, into the desert. This latter choice was not a road, just sand and it had it's dangers. Stray too far from the poles and you were in soft sand. It was no easy ride, and no-one slept, because at times we had to 'bounce' the bus along over the small dunes. It was guaranteed that when we arrived at the palace compound to start work that we were all wide awake.
At 6am we used to wear our long trousers, jumpers, sometimes our overcoats, but always the standard Kuwait Army issue headdress and badge. By 10am we were stripped down to shorts and a shirt, and by midday it was shorts only, because the temperature used to rise to over 100 degrees. If you were working out in the 'open' at this time you made sure that your metal toolbox was in the shade, otherwise your tools were too hot to handle.

Our work in Kuwait was to maintain and repair all this British equipment located in the garage and workshop compound, 23 Chieftain Tanks, an Armoured recovery tank, various armoured cars, and assortment of artillery pieces, general purpose trucks, landrovers and ancillary equipment. One garage accommodated all the tanks, into the other big garage went all the landrovers, leaving all the other vehicles and equipment in rows across the compound. The workshop had a fully equipped and modern hydraulic lifts for maintenance of what had been the Sheik's own private fleet of vehicles.

And so we settled down to a routine of inspection, test and repair as necessary. Some days to break the routine we would take smaller vehicles out of the compound and into the desert surrounding the palace. We even fashioned spears out of obsolete metal rods and we would go on a lizard hunt. This was usually a futile but fun activity, because we never caught a lizard as they were always too fast for us and managed to disappear below ground before we got near them, only to reappear from another hole further away.

We took a tank out once after some repairs had been carried out to check it was okay, but the driver made the mistake of doing a 'neutral' turn in soft sand and one of the drive tracks broke free, and he almost ran the tank off the end of the broken track. So, our next job was to refit the track 'in situ'. This calls for the biggest spanner that you have ever seen, it was about 4 feet long, but it was needed to release and reset the track tensioners. Firstly the broken track was laid out to the rear of the tank and in line with the rollers, a rope was then attached to the front end of the track and passed along the side of the tank on the sand. The rope was then passed over the front idler sprocket and returned to the rear of the tank over the top of the upper rollers. Then the rope was wound around the rear drive sprocket. I was given the task of holding the end of the rope at the drive sprocket, and to the amusement of the other mechanics I was told to put both my feet on the side of the sprocket. This meant that I was stood parallel to the ground with only the rope to hold onto. The engine was re-started, and a gear was engaged and the sprocket started to rotate, along with me as well. As the rope started to take the strain of pulling the broken track under the tank, some comedian shouted "More Revs" and the sprocket started to rotate faster with me spinning at the centre. When the track finally reached the drive sprocket the 'stop' command was given, and, I duly dropped to the sand in a dizzy heap to the raucous laughter from all the other mechanics. The links of the track were refitted in the track and it was driven back to the compound with one still dizzy passenger.

It was not long after this that one of the tank mechanics had been working on another tank's engine, and in order to do this he had to rotate the gun turret 90 degrees to the left to gain access via the engine covers. Having completed his work the mechanic then decided to drive the tank around the inside of the compound, but had forgotten to reset the turret in the forward position. Near the entrance to the compound was the Arab soldiers tin hut, and as the tank drove past the hut, the extended gun barrel, which was still pointing left, sliced through the hut structure, the occupants were seen suddenly flinging themselves out of the windows, before the roof collapsed. The driver of the tank was oblivious, and had to be told afterwards.

On another occasion whilst I was working within the garage bays of the compound, the sky began to get darker. Then a drumming sound started, and got louder by the minute. Not knowing what this was, I went outside the bay and was greeted by a plague of locusts. They were everywhere, millions of them. The bay roofs were painted green, hence the drumming sound as they landed upon it. Some small trees that were stood in the compound suddenly became black and thick, then just as quickly they became thinner and disappeared. All the foliage had gone, leaving only the bare bark. Within minutes it was all over and the noise reduced and it became lighter again. The only people who had remained out in this storm were the Arab guards, who had been catching the locusts and were later seen roasting them on an open fire before they ate them.

This a letter that I wrote to my family in 1962, after we had all been invited to a Sheik's end of Ramadan Feast whilst serving in the Kuwait. .

Sheik Mabarak's Palace

On entry through a highly floodlit archway serving as the Main Gate, we drove down a narrow roadway overhung by all kinds of trees, beneath the trees were beautiful beds of flowers, some already in full bloom.
After travelling for about three quarters of a kilometre we drove into the car park to the right of the main entrance to the Palace proper.

Behind the car park were three separate houses belonging to the three sons of the Sheik Mabarak. The Elder Mabarak, or father is now in disgrace and has removed himself to a palace in the Lebanon.

Walking from the coach to the archway of the main door we climbed up marble steps and passed through marble pillars, the floor now being a marble mosaic of all colours. The doors were of black and gold iron work, the large handles being of gold.

The doors give way to a small fully carpeted hallway or foyer, in which several of the Sheik's personal bodyguard were standing. We passed through a second doorway, and we were in another hall in which prayer mats had been laid down for the use of the Sheik and those of his guests who wished to make use of them. Again the floor was fully carpeted in beautiful Persian carpets, the colours were numerous, and the patterns were beyond belief, truly beautiful. Around the sides of the hall were several small tables with an assorted array of small statuettes and ornaments, of silver, marble, gold and polished woods.

We turned left here and entered the main room or the Sheik's main reception hall. As the Father Mabarak was not present in the household, the elder son received the guests. He was seated at the far end of the hall or the head of the hall. Along the sides of the hall his guests would seat themselves in positions of seniority with the Sheik at the head.

Again the floor was fully carpeted, the main colour being emerald green, In the centre of the floor three large round tables were placed, they were made of an array of polished woods with marble centres and gold edged legs, and gold feet. On the top of the three tables were displayed large vases of fresh flowers.

Stretching around the whole of the sides of the hall were numerous couches coloured green and with gold trimmed arm rests.

Placed at intervals in front of the couches were mirror topped tables with gold cigarette boxes and ash trays in large dishes as sets. Also on each table were small plates of dates covered with serviettes, to be eaten later.

The sides of the hall were all glass windows looking out in various directions over the gardens to the left, to the head of the hall a view out over the sea and to the right over more gardens.

Between the windows at intervals were eighteen pillars of white marble with floral tops in gold. In front of each pillar and hanging off the walls were eighteen chandeliers of glass and bespectacled with gold, each glass stood in a gold holder electrically lit.

Hanging from the main ceiling were six larger chandeliers of the same type as before, but, towards the head of the hall. Above one of the tables hung the most beautiful and magnificent and largest chandelier I have ever seen. It hung about fifteen feet from the ceiling and at the base was about twelve feet in diameter, it had layer upon layer of candles with gold bespectacled into the glass. I estimated well over one hundred and fifty bulbs atop of the candles. As yet it was not lit up, but when it was switched on, later in the evening, it caused a complete silence and gasps in the room, a sight truly never to be forgotten, and probably never to be experienced again.

At the top of the main chandelier were two large rings of eight positioned stars adding to the glitter. All persons upon entering the hall would walk about halfway up the centre of the hall, salute the Sheik, and then to be seated on the couches.

At quarter to six the evening gun was sounded and the Ramadan Fast was broken until sunset the next day. The Sheik arose and walked down the hall and led the way out of the room.

We entered the dining hall through a doorway on the left. The sight alone made us hungry. There were tables laid out with silver platters stacked high with fruit of all kinds. Down the centre of the tables were other large platters laid out with half goats placed on their sides on a bed of rice. Generally dispersed about the tables were plates and bowls of various spices and savouries. Placed in front of each person was a plate with knife, fork and spoon. The Kuwaiti does not use any cutlery at all, he uses his right hand to eat with, and only his right hand and we were instructed to do the same.

In front of myself was a platter with the half goat upon it, and around the base of the platter all the cooked

intestines and organs were placed. I tried with my right hand to break off a piece of goat, but had to be helped by one of the attending servants. It was delicious. I also tried some of the honey coated items which were also nice to eat. Each of us was poured a glass of milk to drink, but when I tried to pick my glass up my greasy fingers slipped on it's straight sides. After several attempts I did manage to get a drink, only to find that the milk was soured goat's milk. The servants brought a hand bowl to wash our hands at the end of the meal.
After the eating, persons left in their own time, as the Sheik had already finished and left the hall.

I took a walk out onto the veranda surrounding the main hall, and I was stood at the top of a stairway facing the sea. In front of me was a large fountain, erected in the middle of a larger pool. There were fourteen little sprays with four larger sprays in a higher position, and then three really high sprays in the centre. It was now dark and the fountain was floodlit from underneath in the big pool, not just one colour but all colours, alternating in the various sprays. Against the shimmer of the sea it was a spectacular sight.

Whilst I stood there alone, I was joined by an Arab who told me that he was the second son of the Sheik, and he told me of his time in education whilst in England. At the end of the evening we all shook hands with all three of our hosts and we boarded our coach to return to our accommodation.

I used to pass my weekends and some evenings babysitting for an English family who worked for the Kuwait Oil Company.

The family lived in the Company Enclave located in a small town settlement about four miles inland from the refinery, and our accommodation. To travel by road it was about eight miles between the two locations. So one night after babysitting till midnight and was unable to get a taxi, I decided to walk back to my billet across the desert. The night sky over the desert is as black as can be, but the refinery had flamer stacks that lit up the sky for miles, and as such acted as a perfect homing beacon for the walk.

The sand was no problem to walk on, but it was a bit undulating, and because of the flames low level lighting, the sand gave the appearance of having lots of black patches in it, these patches being dips in the sand, sometimes only a few inches deep but not always, as I was to find out.

Walking directly towards the flame stacks, a black area appeared before me and it was getting broader with each step, when suddenly, I had the sense to stop, only to find myself staring down at what must have been a very large chasm in the ground, and I was on the edge of it. I stepped back and decided my only course of continuing was to carefully walk around it. As I did so, another large shadow appeared before me, this time above the ground level, but I could not avoid walking towards it, otherwise I would have ended up walking back to where I had come from. The shadow got closer, and as the light was getting brighter, only to reveal that I was walking towards a small Arab village. It had a track passing through it in the direction of the refinery, so I thought it better to use this track rather than have to walk around the perimeter of the village. So I quietly entered the village.

All was going well and I felt confident that I had not disturbed anyone, when suddenly out of the corner of my left eye I sensed a movement. The next thing I knew was that an Arab was jumping at me and grabbing me. Then, came a hefty thump against the two of us, and the Arab spun me around and at the same time he was shouting. In a second it was over, and he released me, so I turned to face him, only to see that he had seized hold of an Alsatian size dog and he was trying to control it. In broken English he told me that he was the night watchman for the village and that the dog was his guard dog. Apparently, on sensing my presence in the village the dog had tried to leap at me, but the watchman just managed to reach me first and the dog had bounced off the pair of us. Nervously I thanked the watchman and stepped lively through the remainder of the village.

I was now well over half way back to the billet compound. The flame stacks were now higher in the sky and more ground was becoming visible by the light, and therefore easier to walk upon.

Seeing the entrance gate to the compound coming into sight about 100 yards ahead of me I felt relief, and thinking of my bed, when I heard a strange noise behind me, I turned and looked behind me only to see that following me were about half a dozen wild pye dogs, their eyes glowing in the reflection of the gas flames. They started to come towards me, and they were growling! The dog's heads were down and I was off - like a rocket! Covering the last few yards to the compound gate in milliseconds, I leapt at the gate, tumbled as I hit the top of it and fell in a heap into the compound. The compound guard fell off his seat at the commotion, he must have been dozing. I stood up, dusted myself off and in an effort to regain my composure I bid him goodnight as I stepped off to my bed, with a sigh of relief.

Whilst in Kuwait we used to receive our 'supplies' at the new Kuwait Airport, which was not yet open to the public. The airstrip was of the latest design, and one of its new innovations was that both ends of the runway were built higher than the centre part. This was intended to give extra lift to taking off aircraft, which we clearly saw when test flights were carried out by both the French Caravelle and the English Comet.

But our aircraft were the ungainly RAF Beverley, and when waiting for it to stop after landing it would come right to the end of the raised runway. One particular delivery was boxes of MT spares and a replacement barrel for one of our tanks. To assist at the unloading our Armourer came along, and as the loading doors at the rear of the aircraft were opened the Aircrew Loadmaster appeared. The Beverly is unusual in that the cargo carrying portion of the plane is shorter than the total fuselage, because the tail units stick out further at the rear by some feet. Underneath this extension of the tail unit is a hidden gantry, which enabled cargos to be swung clear of the cargo bay.

Using the gantry under the tail, it was planned to off load the tank barrel directly onto the platform of our truck. Unfortunately our Arab driver drove too close for comfort to the plane and was ordered away, because any contact would automatically ‘ground’ the plane.

A debate followed between our Armourer and the Loadmaster as to where to place the gantry slings on the barrel. This has to be done carefully as the bulk of the weight is at one end of the barrel, and inspite of its nature and size caution has to be exercised.

As the Loadmaster swung the barrel out of the cargo bay of the aircraft, something happened to make the barrel slip out of the carrying sling, and the barrel dropped onto the runway. Because the aircraft was at the high end of the runway the barrel started to roll down the slope gaining momentum as it went. Like an excerpt from a comedy film, both the Armourer and the Loadmaster ran after the rolling barrel shouting “Stop that Barrel”.

On another occasion I was detailed to travel to the new airport to collect a crated item, I was accompanied by a Lcpl on this task.

This particular item turned out to be a large heavy crate, but it would fit into the back of our Jeep. Having collected the crate we drove it back to our base where it was offloaded, and we were given the instruction to open it. To the dismay of my Lcpl it contained a War Graves Commission Headstone for a soldier who had died in Kuwait prior to our arrival. But the look on the Lcpl's face was that of utter shock, as the headstone was engraved as the same name as his own.

The tanks and armoured vehicles in our charge were from units based in Aden or Bahrain, we were given 48hours notice one day that the Commanding Officer of one of the Tank Regiments was coming to check his vehicles. On hearing this we reacted in the usual military fashion – Panic!

We had been doing a good job of work, but urgent action was needed to make matters look better. The decision was taken to 'bull' everything by coating it with grease. Taking out a Number One Burner it was set up in the yard, foraging parties set off to find all the grease and thick oil that could be found. Large cooking pots were placed on the Burner and we began to 'brew up' an evil mixture of hot oil and grease.

Next, we acquired as many rags and paint brushes as we could find. With cans of our 'brew' we each set off upon the equipment, coating every metallic surface with a liberal coating of the evil mixture. Headlights, hubs, handles and hatches, the tanks got particular attention as they would be the focus of the visit.

On the appointed day the CO duly arrived dressed in his khaki dress uniform (KDs), and he headed for the tanks, climbing up onto the first one he reached the top of the turret. The hatches were open and he stood astride the aperture ready to descend into the tank, only quicker than he anticipated. We had done a good job with the 'brew', and as the CO attempted to descend into the tank, he disappeared at the rate of six feet a second into the bowels of the tank. Moments later his head stuck out of the hatch and he had to be lifted out still dizzy from his rapid descent. His smart KD was now glistening with 'brew'.

The inspection later continued, only this time he was wearing coveralls and gloves, and he was more wary of where he went. Too embarrassed to admit what had happened to him, we did get a satisfactory report.

In 1962 The Sheik Abdullah was receiving £6,000,000 a week from the revenue of the oil that Kuwait produced. The Sheik kept £2,000,000 as his personal income, £2,000,000 went to his Government and the final £2,000,000 was used for the development of his country. In comparison, I, at this point, was earning just over £6 per week.

I look back with contentment on the months that I spent working there, in the Kuwait Army, and as a souvenir of my time I still have my Arab headdress and the cap badges that we used to wear in this secret little army.

All good things come to an end and in the early summer of 1962, we 'initial volunteers' were replaced by more 'regular' members, who were to continue the work.
The return to Aden was unexciting. The only good thing was that having now completed half of my term of posting I was due for some leave, the choice I was given

was a month in Mombasa or a flight back to the UK, I choice to return to the UK to see my Wife. In those days flights from Aden went via Malta and then to Stanstead Airport in Essex. My Wife had temporarily moved to my parent's house in London. We had an enjoyable leave together, until the telegram arrived one day to tell me to report to Victoria Coach station the same day. I was out shopping when the telegram arrived, but I opened it on my return, read it with amazement, it was far too late for me to meet the appointed schedule. So I phoned the contact number given and was told to report, but was redirected to my REME Depot instead, as I had missed my flight, allegedly.

As to be expected I was 'charged' with failing to report for my flight, but the OC accepted my explanation and the charge was dropped. I remained at the Depot for a couple of weeks before a return flight to Aden was arranged for me.

My flight coincided with my 21st Birthday and my wife had brought a cake to the Airport for me. I shared my cake with the Civilian aircrew, who in return treated me to a large whisky, I don't remember much of the flight after that.

Back in Aden I was posted to 653 Light Aircraft Squadron LAD, Army Air Corps, based at Falaise, Little Aden. It was only a small detachment of Vehicle Mechanics, a Sergeant, Lcpl and myself, our Office was a large crate situated in the vehicle compound, our workshop was the desert sand.

The prime concern of the unit was the Light Aircraft, Austers and Beavers, with Alouette helicopters. There mechanics had large hangers to work in. Occasionally, when the Royal Navy's Aircraft Carriers HMS Bulwark or HMS Eagle came to port, there used to be a detachment sent to our airfield with their Westland helicopters for a short period.

We were all accommodated in billeted huts at Falaise Camp, whilst the airstrip and hangers were a mile or so further in land in open country. Access to which was only obtainable along a raised narrow rough track, to avoid flooding by the local tides.
The Army Air Corps in 1962 was administered by the Royal Artillery, with other supporting Corps to fulfil all the other necessary tasks.
One day one of our Gunners returned from a detail to Steamer Point in a 1 ton pick up truck and he had brought with him a Baboon Ape that he had taken off some Arabs who were mistreating it. It must have been one of the ferrel apes that lived on the upper reaches of the Shamsam. The Baboon was chained to the open canopy rails at the rear of the truck and he was swinging about quite happily, but he did have an attitude problem. The Gunner, a Glaswegian, was certainly a match for the Baboon's attitude, as he didn't take any hassle from the animal.

We were billeted at this time in Twyneham huts at Falaise Camp, Little Aden, and having got permission to keep the animal, our Scot 'acquired' some large crates which he converted into a small hut for it. A telegraph pole was attached to the top of the crates and fitted horizontally to a post to form a perch. All this was placed outside the front of our hut on waste ground not far from the camp perimeter barbed wire fence.

As the weeks went by the baboon, now named Jock, became quite a personality. To restrain Jock a small leather belt had been fastened around his waist and this was initially attached to a rope which was tethered to his cage.

Jock used to entertain us by playing on his perch or by running around to the limits of his rope. He eventually formed a circumference in the sand of his limits. We knew that we could approach this circumference with safety as long as we stayed outside of it, but if we entered the area we did so at our peril. At night wild pye dogs used to sneak through the perimeter wire fence and try to steal Jock's food, but were wary of Jock's presence. The dogs knew Jock was tethered and so they used to approach him as close as possible, but not within the limits of the rope. But Jock was canny, he used to take hold behind his back of the last foot of the rope, and hold it as slack behind him, making the rope appear to be shorter than it actually was. A dog would approach Jock and tease him on the rope, and they would stand almost nose to nose, when Jock would suddenly release the concealed rope and surge forward, catching the aggravating dog unawares. Jock was now able to grab the dog by the head, the dogs never let him do it a second time.

Returning to the billet one lunch time after work, we returned to chaos. Jock had bitten through his rope tether and was running loose about the camp. Everyone wanted to join in the fun and games of trying to catch him. Running between the Huts Jock was eventually chased towards the Cookhouse area, where he entered the open doors of the dinning room. The mealtime has started and the dinning room was half full of diners. Jock, now confused, leapt up onto the tables and was jumping from one table to another, to the dismay of the diners. The chasers now entered the dinning room, and Jock was trapped, so he headed over the tables to the rear of the room to the hot plates where all the food was laid out. Up onto the hotplate Jock sprang, only to literally to start 'hot footing' along the surface with the hot meals.

Until at the end he came to the pudding section, where large trays of cold custard and jam tart stood. After the heat of the hotplate the coolness of the cold custard was a relief to Jock, he stood and then sat down in the trays. The cookhouse was now in uproar, the irate cooks now adding to the commotion. Jock was now cornered, he was being approached on one side by the pursuers and on the other by the cooks. For his defence Jock chose to use the custard tart to fight off his captures, by the handful yellow globules began flying through the air in all directions.

The atmosphere became that of a bun fight, with Jock at the centre and everyone else joining in. But it had to end and eventually Jock was recaptured by our Scot, who dragged Jock screaming from the cookhouse back to his cage. From then on Jock was fitted with a chain in lieu of the rope. It was weeks before the Cooks spoke to us again.

One of the technicians in our hut had bought a motorbike and was showing it off to us all by riding around the camp. Jock took a liking to this bike, so one afternoon when the technician was dressed in his white shorts and shirt ready for a trip into town, he decided at the last minute to give Jock a ride on the pillion of the bike within the camp. Jock was duly placed on the seat behind the rider and they set off at a moderate speed. Jock was clinging to the rider and enjoying the experience. Five minutes later the bike came back into view, but the rider was not smiling, and on stopping he told Scot in no uncertain terms to 'Get that animal off my bike', which Scot did. Everyone had come out of the hut to see what all the commotion was about, and the rider sat fuming on his bike. It wasn't until the rider stood up and swung his leg off the bike that we all saw a large yellow stain on the seat of his shorts. Jock had been too excited by the ride.

Travel to the airstrip from the camp each day was by truck along the raised rough track, which was subjected to flooding twice yearly with the Spring and Autumn tides. During the day the airstrip and it's hangers were occupied by servicemen working, but at night the area was normally quiet, with only the usual six man guard on patrol.

The airstrip consisted of two large hangers in which were the repair workshops and storage of the light aircraft and helicopters. Alongside the hangers between

the hangers were the Administration and Workshop Offices. To one side of one hanger was the Motor Transport compound, with it's smaller workshop and the unit vehicle park. It was in this compound, with only it's barbed wire surround, was the tent which acted as the Guard accommodation for the night.
The hangers at night were illuminated by arc lights from each of the buildings corners, which meant that the hangers themselves were in the shadows, the side compound only had reduced lighting.

When on guard, two of us were always on duty, we soon discovered that as long as you stayed close to the hangers, and under the beam of the arc lights, when on patrol, that you could not be seen from a distance.

It was one night when on guard that we spotted a single set of headlights moving along the rough track towards the airstrip. Movement at night along this track at night without lights was impossible.

The lights came closer, and duly stopped at about 100yds from the hangars. In the still of the night we could hear car doors open and close, but could not see anything in the darkness. All went quiet, and we stayed hidden in the shadows.

On first sight of the oncoming lights we had warned the remainder of the guard and they had stood to, again in the shadows. We were all armed, and had ammunition in our pouches, but not in the weapons.

There was no sign of who had come in the mystery vehicle, but we knew that the hangers could be under observation. Our guard was spread along the front of the hangers and compound area spread out over a distance of about 100yds. On the order of the guard commander we all briefly stepped from the shadows forward into the arc of our lights, so that we could be seen, then quickly stepped back again into the shadows. This 'visible' show must have surprised our visitors, as they probably thought the airstrip was unattended. Because the next we heard was the vehicle restart and it drove off back down the track towards the camp.

As soon as this happened we contacted the camp on the telephone, and the guard at the camp formed a road block to stop the vehicle as it exited from the track.

We later heard that a vehicle had been stopped with two Arabs and searched, and it was found that they had been carrying weapons with them concealed in the vehicle. Quite what their intentions had been we do not know, but it proved a valuable lesson to us, because parked in the compound just behind the guard tent was a petrol bowser used for refuelling the aircraft, and it was filled with 2000 gallons of aviation fuel. An easy target had any action taken place.

Working at the airstrip, one day we all heard a large aircraft approaching, on going to the front of the hangers, we could see in the distance a double rotor RAF helicopter (a Belvedere). Underneath the helicopter was slung the fuselage of one of our Squadron Auster aircraft, but without it's wings. The RAF had been upcountry and recovered the Auster and was bringing it back to the Squadron Workshop for repair.

A crowd gathered to watch the delivery, including our Commanding Officer. The helicopter slowly came to hover in front of the hangers at about a height of 60 feet. Now stationary it started to lower the Auster on it's winch. When the Auster was about 40 feet from the ground it was suddenly released and it plummeted to the ground. Bouncing on it's undercarriage, it rose into the air a few feet, then the fuselage snapped in the middle and it fell again to the tarmac landing on it's nose and tail. But with it's broken back in the air. Like most things dramatic it all appeared to happen in slow motion and somewhat gracefully. Silence descended upon the onlookers.

The Belvedere now backed off a short distance and then landed, our CO sprang forward and demanded to know from the Winchman what had happened? He replied "I got the order to cut sir". "From whom?" demanded the CO.

The Winchman replied "From the flight deck, sir".
Our CO jumped onboard the helicopter and made his way straight to the flight deck. When our CO asked the Pilot about the order to cut, the Pilot merely said "Sorry, old chap, I coughed into the microphone, it must have sounded like I said cut".

It came to pass that a new Sergeant Major (who had just been posted to our unit from an Anti-Aircraft Battery of the Royal Artillery) attended his first morning parade of all personnel, His first words of command on parade were “653 Light Anti-Aircraft Squadron – Shun!”. To everyone’s amusement, but his own.

All the time I was in Aden I maintained my interest in photography, which came in very useful at times. Members of 653 had a couple of go-carts that they regularly raced at other units, usually at weekends. So I started to travel with the unit team, and I took photos of the events and prize presentations afterwards. It was at these meetings that I met an RAOC Captain who took an interest in my photographic work, and when the opportunities arose we used to discuss photography. Later, in West Germany I was to meet this Captain again.

I mentioned ‘side lines’ from the photography as being a means of raising extra funds for me, one of the most lucrative tasks was when I ‘borrowed’ from my Arab friend sets of Japanese slides of naked models. These I used to project onto the billet wall, much to the enjoyment of all in attendance, then I would photograph each projection, after which I printed postcards for all those who wished to buy them, there was never a lack of willing customers. I would then return the slides to the Arab along with a complimentary set of photos, which he was delighted to receive.

One place in Aden that held an interest for me was the Tawahi Water Tanks situated in the walls of the Shamsan at the back of Crater City. Not always considered a safe place to go to.

These Water Tanks were discovered in the 19th Century, but their history is not known. They were a series of vertical walls built up the crevasse of the steep side of the volcano, as dams, with large holding Tanks at the base. The total amount of water that the tanks could hold was estimated to be in the millions of gallons. But, sadly through neglect and drought were no more than an ornament. But I found them good for photographic shots.

One disappointment for me whilst serving in South Arabia was that I failed to qualify for the award of the General Service Medal (with the South Arabia Bar). MOD in it's wisdom decided to cease the issue of the GSM in 1961, and change it to the New Campaign Service Medal. But the transition period between 1961 and 1964 did not apply to Aden for some strange reason, and has been contested ever since. Although places like Borneo continued to qualify.

June 1963 my tour of duty in Aden came to a close, and I was presented with the following document to send home to my family:

This is a copy of the standard letter that Soldier's due for return to the UK used to send to their relatives as a 'Squaddy' joke: Teeny Weeny Airways, TWA, is the Army Air Corps.

Teeny Weeny Airways
Based in Aden

Official Notice of Return

Issued in warning this .... day of 1963.

To all the neighbours, relatives and friends of...........................

1. Very soon the above named individual will once again be in your midst. It is your duty to help this dehydrated and demoralized victim to take his place once again as a human being, with his sudden freedom and liberty in society. You must make allowances for his actions, all caused by his being imprisoned in this crude environment, which has been his miserable lot for the past two years. He will be suffering from Adenitis, his habits are Eastern, all caused by too much sun.

2. In making your joyous preparations to welcome him back to organised civilised society you must make some allowances for his actions and his habits. A few suggestions that would help to cultivate and civilise him once again are hereafter suggested:

a. Lock up all females between nine and ninety.

b. fill the fridge with beer, lots of it, remember he will only drink it cold out of cans. Glasses are unknown to him.

c. Buy the biggest mug you can find, and constantly fill it with an unknown substance to him – Coffee. Do not give him Tea, he now hates it.

d. Make his bed comfortable for his afternoon sleeps.

e. Remove all mothballs from his clothes, and reminds him to put them on.

3. At mealtimes please excuse his table manners. At first he will only eat with his right hand, try to gently introduce him to a spoon and then a knife and fork. His left hand he keeps to himself!

Try to keep calm when he pours gravy on his desert and then mixes it with his peaches and mash potatoes.
When he 'belches' look pleased, as it means he likes your cooking.

NEVER – feed him Lancashire hot pot, cottage pie, savoury mince, treacle tart, bananas or corned beef. He's had his fill.

When serving up such rarities as fresh bread and real butter, milk or vegetable, do not be disgusted if he goes at it like a wild beast. When he mutters between mouthfuls, “Tomum mungeria” it means “Very good food”.

When he arrives at the station, send someone to guide him home. When he greets you with “ Salam Alihkum, keif halleck” He’s pleased to see you. On boarding a bus, buy his ticket for him or else he will attempt to argue his fare with the conductor.

For the first few weeks go with him when he goes shopping, or else he will end up in trouble by trying to barter a price for each item he wants to buy.

When you take him to the cinema for the first time, tell him he doesn’t need to take goggles and a blanket. Also tell him he pays on entry and not after the first reel.
When at home tolerate his squatting cross legged on the mat, or walks around only wearing a towel, throwing his blankets on the floor and sleeping there as well.

When he attempts to set fire to his bed, don’t be alarmed, he’s trying to get rid of the bed bugs.

When woken up and he finds his shoes are not cleaned, his bed is not made, or a mug of hot tea are not brought to him in the mornings, he will start shout “Chico” (small boy who acts as servant) the best idea is to dress the youngest member of the family in a dirty towel, and smear him all over with soot and run as would a young Somali lad to his bedside to do his master’s bidding.
When he’s taken out for the first time, explain to him in your best Pidgeon English that books are available at Bookshops, what a double decker bus is, a tree, grass, a

train, the local fish & chip shop and of course, the local pub.

When it rains for the first time since his home coming do not be surprised if he grabs his trusty towel and rushes forth to the garden carrying all the bowels, buckets and containers that he can find. He will then just stand and look up at the rain, and he will probably start to have a wash. No, he's not gone mad, so don't call the Psychiatrist, remember that rain is unknown to him. Just gently take him to the bathroom and let him play.

In fear of your life, never ask him if he liked it here! UGH! Never mention going to the seaside and sand, sunny days or Arabs.
Just bear in mind that below that rugged tanned exterior there beats a heart of gold. Treasure this, it is the only thing of value he has left. Treat him with kindness, tolerance and an occasional can of beer, and he will be your friend for life and his rehabilitation will soon be complete.

-o-o-o-o-o-o-o-o-o-

My return to the UK was uneventful, apart from the fact that when I boarded a London Bus, I was mistaken for a foreigner, because of the dark colour of my skin. My Wife had returned to Scotland, so I took the overnight train to Aberdeen. Again we had an enjoyable leave, except that in July in Scotland I really felt the cold. I was sent instructions to report to my Depot for onward posting.

Chapter Five
(West Germany 1963 – 68)

July 1963, I again reported to my Depot REME, by now the Army was modernizing, and I was to be re-equipped with the new No 2 Uniform, the battledress had now been withdrawn from service, and replaced by a suit they called a Combat Dress. I had a new raincoat (no greatcoat), No2 Uniform consisting of a modern style jacket and trousers to suit, No 2 Headdress cap and a pair of shoes, new shirts, pullover and a suitcase. The trusty old .303 Lee Enfield rifle was now replaced by the new 7.62 self loading rifle (SLR).

I was transported to Standstead Airport for my flight to Germany. Here a problem arose and instead of sending me to Gutersloh Airport I was sent to Hannover instead. Arriving at Hannover the Movements Staff allocated me some overnight accommodation in a barracks in the city. Next morning I was issued with a rail warrant and directions of how to get to Lippstadt, my new posting. The German Rail system was very efficient, and my directions were reasonable, which was a good thing because I neither read nor understood any German language at the time. Transport was waiting for me at the station and I was driven to my new barracks.

The unit I was to be attached to was 22 Signal Regiment, Royal Signals, in the REME LAD Workshop. The LAD consisted of about 25 REME and RAOC personnel plus German Civilian Trades, a Welder,

Carpenter, Mechanics and a Coach Trimmer all with their own Foreman Supervisor, Interpreter.

The Signal Regiment itself consisted of 3 Squadrons (Companies) of various types of Signal Equipment, plus an Headquarter Company for overall administration. The Regiment had about 200 vehicles, of mixed types, including some armoured and generator trailers.

One of the German characters of the LAD was a Welder, a big man of jovial character, but who spoke little English.

This Welder used to work at the side of the trailer repair bay, his usual trick to greet new arrivals was to get them to hold a length of metal whilst he balanced the other end on the vice, to weld it. In those days soldiers were still issued with the Ammo Boots with steel toe and heel plates, and unknowingly whilst obliging to hold the piece of metal, the newcomer was stood on a metal plate strategically placed on the floor. With the soldier's attention drawn to the welding at the vice by an accomplice, The German used to sneak behind the unsuspecting soldier, with another electric welder and he would 'spot' weld the soldier's boots to the metal plate. To the amusement of all present the victim then had to unlace his boots and step out of them, walk to his own toolbox in his stocking feet collect his hammer and chisel to release his boots from the plate.

One memorable day The German Welder was given a trailer support leg to repair, and it needed some grinding off on the grind wheel which was located at the rear of the work bay. Six feet from the grinding machine was the paraffin bath which we used to wash and clean greasy items, and it contained highly inflammable fluids. The Welder having completed his repair took the metal leg to the grinder to take off the surplus. Happy in his work he was grinding away on the machine with showers of sparks flying over his shoulder. These sparks landed in the paraffin bath and ignited it. The German was oblivious, and he kept on grinding away, with the flames behind him getting bigger. Warning shouts were given by personnel in the bay, but he was unable to hear for the noise of his grinding. Using foam extinguishers we managed to dowse the flames in the bath. It was then that the German decided to turn around, totally oblivious to what had happened.

We used to take our Tea Break in the work bay, and all our brew kit, including our metal mugs were located on a wooden bench at the back of the bay. To our amusement one day the Welder's mug had a hole drilled in the bottom of it and it was screwed to the wooden bench top. The mug was then duly filled with tea and the Welder came across to the bench to retrieve his brew, to roars of laughter when he tried to lift it.

Each evening when we finished work, we tidied up the work bay and this included placing all our metal toolboxes in a pile against the wall. Here the Welder sought his revenge. The next morning we entered the workshop, and found that all our toolboxes were stacked where we had put them, but all the corners of the boxes had been welded together!

We also had one of the last National Serviceman, another Welder, serving out his Conscription time, and one day a Bedford truck came to the workshop for repairs to its damaged door, which had a big dent in it. This Welder was given the task of repairing it. Two hours later the Welder reported to the Workshop Office that the job was done. The Officer Commanding the Workshop overheard him and said "Surely not that quick", and he stepped outside to check the vehicle. There it was, all nice and smooth, not a sign of any damage and it had been given a new coat of olive drab paint as well. The OC could not believe it, so he called us all over to see this repaired marvel. "This" said the OC to all in attendance "Is how to carry out a job". At the same time the OC was tapping the 'new panel' with his swagger stick. There was a ripping sound and the tip of the stick disappeared into the panel, a look of amazement on everybody's faces. On closer examination it was found that the Welder had stuck a sheet of brown paper over the damaged door panel then he had painted it over to make it look good, which it did until the OC put his stick through it!

Because I was now over 21 years old I was able to have my wife and family with me and with Christmas fast approaching and the preparations were well under way. The decorations had been made and some had been bought, but, we lacked the most important item – a Christmas Tree.

It was the families first Christmas in Germany and the first in a Married Quarter, more reasons for a Family celebration after so long a separation.

A trip to the NAAFI was all that was needed to order the necessary tree, so off we all set, and the children were full of anticipation.

The Sales Assistant filled out the necessary Order Form and asked me what height? I said five foot would suffice. I duly paid the deposit and was given the collection date for the tree.

When the day arrived I drove to the NAAFI in our estate car, thinking this would be ample room for the tree.
At the NAAFI I was given the tree that I had ordered – it was longer than the car! I queried the size of the tree against the order, and the Form was produced, stating that I had requested a tree of the size supplied. Obviously there had been a mistake, either in what I had said or what was heard by the sales assistant, because the tree was three times larger than expected. For the tree had been ordered from the supplier in metres and not in feet, a breakdown in Anglo German understanding. But we definitely had the biggest tree we've ever had. Never to be forgotten.

Because of my interest in photography I was engaged occasionally as the Regimental Photographer. This entailed that apart from functions I would accompany the Commanding Officer and take photos at his request. The CO was a stickler for good camouflage and military training, this meant that whilst on exercises he frequently told me to take photos for him so that he could highlight good and bad practices of the soldiers. When 'in the field' the unit was scattered in all sorts of locations, so the CO used to travel by helicopter, if possible. One time this involved overflying Osnabruck Zoo, and the CO suggested that I take a few photos. My camera, with it's telephoto lens, had been resting on the helicopter floor, so as the helicopter banked for a shot, I picked up my camera and turned it downwards, only to have the heavy lens fall off the camera and descend rapidly to earth somewhere within the zoo. I never did hear if any damage had been caused by this 2lb lump of glass, but could visualize the effect it could have caused when it reached the ground.

As mentioned previously, whilst in Aden I had met an RAOC Captain, with whom we shared an interest in photography, it was whilst I was on Exercise in Germany that I met this Captain again, and he enquired if I was still involved in photography, I said that I was, and that I had been used as the Regiment's Photographer.

He himself had been posted as Publicity Officer to 4 Div HQ Public Relations Unit. He revealed to me that he needed a 'still' photographer for some assignments that he was going to do in July/August. It was duly arranged with my unit that I be temporarily attached to his unit for that six week's period.

So it was that I ended up with the Public Relation Unit, as the Official Army Photographer in Belgium and Northern France for the 50th Anniversary of the outbreak of the First World War.

The assignment was to record all the celebrations that were happening locally. The key event was on the 4th

August when a 13 Pounder Gun was brought from the Imperial War Museum. This particular Gun had been used to fire the first shot back in 1914 by the Royal Horse Artillery, only this time, a Lance Bombardier (now a Pensioner) who had been a member of this Gun's Crew in 1915, was going to re-enact the shot again with the assistance of ceremoniously dressed members of the King's Troop RHA, on the same spot of 1914.

At the appointed time, the gun was prepared, and the assembled International Press Corps of about 30 photographers waited, along with dignitaries and members of the public. I was stood prepared with two cameras, one my own, the other belonged to the Army, and I used a stack of crates as a support for the cameras.

The Pensioner sat at the gun, and prepared to fire the 'shot'. But, in the intervening years he had forgotten how strong the trigger mechanism was, he tried once and all the cameras including one of mine 'clicked' in anticipation of getting an 'action shot' of the gun firing. Within a second the Pensioner reacted and successfully pulled the trigger. The gun fired, but it was only my second camera that had caught the shot. The moment having past there was a cry "Did anyone get the shot?" I said that I had been successful and a man came across and asked if he could have the film. To which my Captain agreed. The man had been a Reporter for Reuter, and it was that evening that my action photo was sent around the News Agencies of the world. My moment of glory over we had more work to carry out.

Also, Families and relatives in the UK had asked for photographs of their relatives graves, so it was that I was in one of the larger cemeteries when I saw a Chelsea Pensioner moving along the rows of headstones. He stopped at one just behind me, and having stood for a moment he came to attention and he saluted the stone, it was then that I saw the tears on his cheeks. Again, I managed to catch another photograph, it was of him at that emotional moment. In all we spent about 10 days in France and Belgium on this assignment.

We next moved onto Alkmaar, in Holland, where a detachment of the Chestnut Troop RHA was visiting the town as part of there annual celebrations. This Unit's visit entailed bringing some of their armoured vehicles and an Army helicopter with them. The idea was to give a display to the townsfolk of the use of the vehicles and the helicopter, which involved a lot of loud bangs, and low flying by the helicopter. That was until the local Policeman turned up on his bicycle calling for a halt in the proceedings, as the local farmers were bitterly complaining the noise of the event was disturbing their cows, and would affect there milking, because Alkmaar is the centre of the cheese industry in Holland. So it was that the British Army was stopped by a local Bobby. It was all taken in good humour, apart from the cows.

In the LAD I spent a lot of time working on and repairing generators and trailers with the occasional armoured car.

By1964 my Trade Classification had been raised to Class 2 and I was considered capable of working by myself. So I was sent on my own on various detachments with the Unit, one of which included a trip to Norway.

The Regiment had recently been supplied with new radio communication equipment, and it was necessary to test it's effectiveness. To do this a series of Radio Stations were to be set up from Norway through to the Middle East. The first Station was to be in Norway at Andelsnes, the second station was to be in Western Germany, the third station down in Bavaria and separate stations were to be used in Italy, Cyprus and the Middle East. For my detachment it meant the long drive up through West Germany (two days), then Denmark, arriving in the evening at the port of Frederikshavn.
Here we had the opportunity to tidy ourselves up for the overnight ferry to Larvik in Norway. We were now parked, all seven vehicles and trailers in the assembly park at the Harbour.

We were already drawing the attention of the other passengers awaiting the ferry, being foreign soldiers in uniform. Then some bright spark decided that he wanted to have an electric shave, in the middle of nowhere. So, he tried to start the generator attached to his vehicle, but with no success, he tried again, still no joy. So as the mechanic I was called over to start the machine, but, unfortunately the driver had flooded the engine and I had to take out the spark plugs of each cylinder to clean and dry them before placing them back into the engine, when it did start. The whole process because it was a 'screened' system had taken nearly half an hour, much to the amusement of our civilian onlookers. To my amazement, all that work was for one electric razor to be plugged in!

Boarding time came and all vehicles entered the waiting Ferry and sailed about dusk. Some of us slept during the crossing, others were a little worse for wear.

Docking at Larvik in the early morning our convoy formed up ready to travel via Oslo all the way up to Andelsnes, which was to be our base for the Exercise.
The road to Oslo in parts was raised above the fields, and it was at one of these points that the driver of one of our Bedford trucks and trailer lost control and both the truck and trailer veered off the road, hit a telegraph pole on the cab front and mounted a very large rock which sheared the back axle of the truck from its springs. A civilian Recovery Vehicle had to requested to retrieve the vehicle and trailer. With the trailer disconnected from the truck, the Bedford then had to be suspended towed to a local Garage where it was arranged for me to stay with it, repair it, then rejoin the Unit at Andelsnes.
The remainder of the Unit continued north, whilst I sorted myself out to carry out the repairs needed. The garage owner was very co-operative, and with the rear end of the Bedford stood upon some supports I was able to remove fully the whole back axle, rebuild the road springs, insert substitute centre pins, then refit the assembles back on the truck. All was progressing well until it came to refitting the braking systems. The hydraulic pipe to the axle had been stretched with the interior pipe only just attached to the outer covering and rendered the rear axle brakes useless. I had to make a clamp to seal this pipe at a strong point to be able to

operate the front axle brakes. The handbrake cable hung like a Chinese washing line, but again I managed to use a series of cable clamps to shorten it to an operable length. The back end of the truck now fixed as far as I could make it, was lowered onto the ground, and with careful testing was found to be useable, albeit with limited braking capacity.

The front of the cab had hit a telegraph pole and had smashed all the panels which needed hammering out as far as possible, but not all could be refitted. But I managed to refit the headlamp, and road lights in suitable places, to be roadworthy, this complete work took me nearly two full days. Having thanked the Garage staff for their help I then set off on the morning of the third day. I had been left a map, directions, and jerry cans of fuel, a selection of rations and some Norwegian cash for the journey. With caution I managed to drive through Oslo, receiving some 'funny looks' from the locals as I did so.

The road North to Andelsnes was the main route northwards, and therefore reasonably easy to follow. By nightfall I had reached Lillehammer, and I parked up for the night and fell asleep wrapped in my sleeping bag in the back of the truck.

Next morning I continued to Dombas where I had to turn west to the coast. It was here that I started to get low on fuel and had to purchase some from a garage.
Between Dombas and Andelsnes I had to descend from the high ground down through the Fiords to sea level, because Andelsnes is on the coast.

To say the least I descended in low gear and with as little use of the brakes as possible, the road was winding with many hair bends, but I was relieved to reach the coast and the Base.

On Arrival I was greeted with relief, but then I had to view the havoc that had been rendered on the other vehicles during their journey. One Landrover had been on its side, another had collided with a civilian truck, and one of the Wireless Station Austins had run into the back of one of our own trailers. What a mess! No wonder they were pleased to see me. Needless to say my next few days were spent hammering and bashing out all the damage, I did get the satisfaction of making as much noise as I could in retaliation.

With all this work completed, I suddenly found myself redundant, because all that was happening, now that the Wireless Stations had been established, and the Exercise had commenced, with only the running of the generators which the Operators were trained to maintain.

So, I asked the OC of the Group if I could go 'walkabout', possibly to the Artic Circle, a distance of about 1200 miles. To my surprise he agreed, and within the hour I set off on foot out of the camp. I was wearing my combat dress, carrying my small pack which contained, a tin of sweets, rice, my washing kit and boot brushes, plus a roll of toilet paper and my ground sheet for bad weather.

A British Uniform in Norway is never ignored, and I was offered numerous lifts on my way north. On the first day I was given a lift by an English speaking Norwegian in his jeep and he took me to Trondheim, where he showed me the upturned keel of the Battleship Tirpitz, and memorials by the side of the road, dedicated to British Commandos who had travelled to these shores and sadly never returned home during the Second World War. He was also kind enough to give me accommodation and food for the night as well.

Being in Norway in August you would think that the weather would be warm, it is during the day, but at night it can fall below freezing especially as you venture further north.

North from Trondheim the road, as such, became a stone pathway except when approaching settlements, where a stretch of tarmac appears, and then reverts to stone on the other side. This is the main road north, and although having traffic it can be intermittent, more trucks than cars.

On my second day of walking I had reached a point only 60km south of the Arctic Circle and was kindly given a lift by two American Geologists, and we arrived at the Artic Circle ten minutes before the Tourist Centre closed at 11pm. So I purchased my signed Visitor's Certificate and took a quick cup of tea before setting off southwards again. The Americans were travelling further north, so I set off on foot into the night.

The Artic sky is still light at this time of year, so visibility was reasonable, the scenery was darkened, so there was little of interest to see, just fir trees and large rocks by the roadside.

In my solitude I half trudged and marched in order to keep up the momentum on the stony surface, it was then that the temperature began to hit me, it was cold! The only way to keep warm was to keep moving, so I did.
After a while flashes of light started to appear behind me, and grew in intensity. Then I heard it, a deep roar, undulating slightly as it grew nearer and then around the bend appeared this truck and trailer, roaring through the night.

I quickly jumped to the side of the road, to get out of it's way, but fortunately the driver had seen me and he slowed, eventually to a stop. Little did I know it but I was about to be given the most hair raising trip of my life. The driver spoke little English, but was polite, he recognised my uniform and was pleased to give me a lift, and I was glad of the warmth of his cab. The engine of the Scania Vabis unit roared into life and through the gears the driver accelerated, the headlights searching into the distance, swinging left and right as the vehicle manoeuvred the bends of the roadway. Then suddenly, the lights peered into oblivion and the road was even shorter, the driver swung the steering wheel and we turned and disappeared into a tunnel. We were on the edge of the fiord travelling at speed through tunnels cut into the rock face. In, out, lights flashing, tunnel entrance, exit, again and again. The driver knew what he was doing, but I was a nervous wreck.

To feel the cold of the night after I had alighted from the truck was a relief. At least I knew that I was still alive. The truck disappeared into the night and I continued my plodding. It was still only 2am and I could feel it getting even colder, and with the cold came stiffness, but I persevered with my marching and rubbing my joints and limbs as I progressed.

Around 6am I came upon a small wooden platform with two large churns of fresh milk awaiting collection. I took the liberty of a mug of milk, as I had only limited provisions with me in my small pack. I felt refreshed having had a drink, but I was tiring of marching, so I looked for a place to rest awhile and found a small gully by the side of the road, into to which I pushed clumps of bracken and small heather bushes to make a bed, onto this I lay my groundsheet. Laying down I pulled the remainder of the groundsheet over me with as much bracken as I could and fell into a fitful sleep, only to be woken an hour later by the milk driver collecting the churns. I was now cold and stiff and again glad of the warmth of a truck cab as we progressed to the next town.

I discovered later that the temperature that night had been below zero, and that I had managed to march nearly 30km. Even today it makes me shiver to think of it!

Further on my journey south I passed the barracks of the Norwegian King's Troop, the ones that wear the black bowler hats and the large feather. Some of these soldiers walked with me for a while as they were curious at seeing a British uniform.

After six weeks the Exercise was over and we returned to Lippstadt. Where to my surprise my adventure to the Artic Circle had been broadcast and published in the Divisional Magazine.

On my return to the Regiment I was asked by the Commanding Officer if I would make a Cine Film recording of the impending visit to the unit by the Senior Signal Officer from NATO.

For this I had to borrow a Cine camera from a German friend and I tried to familiarize myself with it. Next I had to prepare a programme of filming which would include the unit's preparation for the visit, the visit itself, which included a Drive Past by vehicles of the unit, and then photograph the Officer's Reception afterwards.

So in the weeks prior to the date, I went around the unit lines and various workshops filming a variety of activities in readiness, which was greeted by all participants as hilarious and with a lot of amateur dramatic antics. During the various rehearsals of the Drive Past I tried to film it from different angles, an attempt to make it less boring than continual filming from one place.

The Unit was paying for all the film used, and I had also borrowed an 8mm Editing machine and splicer.

Having done all the pre-visit filming, I now had to concentrate on the day of the visit itself, so I carefully planned my 'filming' positions and even timed how long it would take me to get from one location to the next. For the arrival of the Officer I planned to be at the Main Gate to film his Inspection of the Guard, then, I would run to the third floor of the HQ Building as it gave a good panoramic view over the Rostrum and the road of the drive past. From here I planned later whilst the Drive Past was proceeding that I would return to ground level to film the left side of the vehicles passing the rostrum, with the saluting base in the background. Only the day previous, during the dress rehearsal, I had stood on the right side of the road to capture the vehicles as they past. My thought was to give an alternating view of the Drive Past when I did the editing.

The day of the Inspection, I was present at the Main Gate when the Officer arrived and having satisfied myself that I had recorded enough of his Inspection of the Guard, I proceeded to the HQ Building. I ran to the third floor only to find that the room from which I wanted access was locked. So I went down to the floor below, and only just set the camera up before the Officer arrived at the Rostrum. The Drive Pass then started, and I continued filming it, until I then returned to ground level and stood by the side of the roadway, where I resumed recording the last of the drive past. Now what could go wrong?

Once the films had been processed, I set about viewing and editing it to create the 'finished' film prior to viewing.

The editing machine that I had borrowed was only a reel to reel machine with a small two inch viewing screen between the reels. The screen was not big enough to view all details as I wound the machine. But, I selected the most prominent lengths of film and duly spliced them together.

My Workshop Officer asked to view the finished film before I gave it to the Commanding Officer. A screen was set up in a darkened corner of the workshop, and a small audience assembled.

Now that I could see in far larger detail the film on the screen, I could see with horror any mistakes that had occurred during the filming.

Comedy of errors. The pre-visit filming of the unit working and preparing for the visit, it included, the paint sprayer who's hose was not connected to the spray machine, a couple of clowns who decided to pull faces and antics in the background, and usual gestures.

But worse was to come. The Inspection of the Guard was okay, but, during my run to the HQ building I must have moved the speed controls on the camera, from fast to slow. This meant that the filming was taken slowly, but the showing was speeded up! With the consequence that when the Officer's car arrived at the rostrum, it did so at speed, the car doors burst open, and the Officer's sprang out in double time. Not only had I moved the speed control I had also change the viewing lens from telephoto to distant. The result was that the car looked in miniature and the officer's looked like ants scurrying about.

Fortunately, whilst filming I had spotted these errors and had reset the camera before filming the next part of the drive past.

In front of the rostrum, but hidden behind a hedge was the Military Band, which provided the accompanying music to the drive, however, the Band Master had to stand at the kerbside so that he could both conduct the band but also to see the signals for the drive past. Even though there had been many practises for the vehicles in driving two abreast past the rostrum, on the day, one of the drivers last control, with the result that he mounted the pavement just where the Bandmaster was standing. On the film it can clearly be seen the vehicle moving and in reaction the Bandmaster literally leaping for his own safety into the hedge.

As I have previously said, during the dress rehearsal, I had filmed the drive past on the right hand side of the road, and on the day I had filmed it from the left side, in order to get alternative viewings after the editing. Unfortunately, the day of the dress rehearsal the weather was sunny and fine, but, on the day of the visit, it was raining! This made my alternative shots, sunny - wet, sunny – wet, the source of more laughter from my viewing audience.

I was relieved when the showing of the film was finished, to everyone's amusement, but my gross embarrassment. Nothing more was said about me showing the film to the Commanding Officer, and I still have it with me to this day, somewhere. After this episode I was nicknamed ‘Movietone’ for the remainder of my time with this unit.

It was during another Exercise in 1964 that I suffered what I can only describe as a Mental Breakdown, my actions were causing concern and I felt ‘unwell’, so much so that I was withdrawn from the Exercise and taken by ambulance to the Medical Centre at Paderborn, where I was examined by a Psychiatrist. I remained in Paderborn for a short period, during further examinations. The outcome was that I was given one of two choices: I could leave the Army on Medical grounds or as it was put to me ‘buck up my ideas and soldier on’. At this point in time I had a wife and two children, and we were solely dependant upon the Service for our home & wages, we did not have any means to start a new life in Civvy Street. I chose to stay in the Army, and I was given medical help for a period afterwards.

I did have an accident in 1965 that has left me with a scar to this day. I was assisting a senior NCO to release a badly wound winch rope on the Scammel Recovery Vehicle, where it needed to be released and unwound, which meant that the rope had to be pulled manually from the vehicle. I was given the task of pulling the rope, and supplied with a pair of staple palmed gloves (as protection) and a large screwdriver to place in the eyelette at the end of the winch rope. The idea was, that with the aid of the screwdriver duly inserted that I could apply pressure to pull the winch rope when the mechanism was released. I stood ready at the rear of the vehicle, when suddenly, instead of releasing the winch rope, it was withdrawn further into the rollers at the rear of the vehicle, taking the screwdriver and my hands with it. When the winch stopped my left hand was trapped along with the screwdriver between the rollers. The screwdriver had sliced into the glove and had guillotined a finger of my left hand. For a moment I stood there, unable to move, and in pain, until I could be released. I was taken straight away to the Medical Centre where my hand was treated, but it meant the removal of my broken wedding ring. For weeks I was unable to work, until the hand healed sufficiently. I still have the scar on my wedding finger, and the wedding ring I had repaired in 2014, never wearing another ring during my service.

Whilst a young Craftsman was busily working away under a vehicle, he was approached by a young Subaltern accompanied by a Sergeant. The Subaltern enquired of the soldier as to what he was repairing? And the Craftsman attempted to reply, only to be interrupted by the Sergeant asking "Did the soldier not usually pay a compliment to an Officer?" (implying a salute). There was a moments' pause, then the Craftsman said "Nice aftershave Sir".

In the Barracks we could clearly hear the sound of the German Police car's siren, Nah Noo! Nah Noo! in the distance, and it was getting closer.

Then, down the road to the Workshop within the Barracks came the Recovery Vehicle, obviously in a rush. The driver was waving to us frantically. "Quick! Quick!" he was shouting "Get this off the back", indicating a large Xmas Tree laid next to the crane. We jumped onto the vehicle and duly offloaded the said tree. The driver then drove off further into the barracks, shouting as he went “Hide it. Quick! I’m being followed”.

As fast as the recovery vehicle disappeared at one end of the road, a German Police car appeared at the other end, approaching rapidly with blue lights flashing. The car came to a halt where we were all stood, and a Provost from the Guard Room stepped out and demanded had we seen the Recovery Vehicle? We unanimously denied any knowledge of the vehicle. The Provost shouted “He’s been nicking Xmas trees and the German Police need to catch him with it”. We stood innocently listening as the Police car drove off continuing the pursuit.

What had happened to the tree? Well, opposite the Workshops on the other side of the road was a planted area of large bushes and small trees. And the Provost and the Police could not ‘see’ the Xmas tree for the all the others. By the time the Police caught up with the driver he was hosing the vehicle down in the Wash Point. Not a tree to be seen!

Later, the ‘hidden’ tree was moved to the Workshop Club were it was duly decorated and added to the Xmas festivities.

In 1965 I was promoted to Lance Corporal (Lcpl) after which followed a posting to 17 Squadron Royal Corps of Transport Workshop REME (LAD) at Rattingen, near

Dusseldorf. 17 Sqn RCT consisted of a mixture of general transport trucks of 4 & 10 tons capacities, Bedfords, AEC and some Leylands.

Whilst serving with the Squadron Workshop, we were on exercise in a farmyard. A new member of the unit was a young naive Craftsman straight out of training, he soon acquired the nickname of Boo Boo.

It was customary during exercises for Officers and senior NCOs to claim all the vehicles for their accommodation, the rest of us had to rough it in the barns. Boo Boo being a first timer, found it difficult 'slumming' down on the hay with all the vermin running about. This came to the attention of the senior Warrant Officer and it was arranged clandestinely amongst all members of the unit for Boo Boo to be called to the Warrant Officer's vehicle. This vehicle was a converted 3 ton truck with steps leading up to the tailgate when opened horizontally. The interior was like an office, but with the addition of a bunk bed for the Warrant Officer.

At the appointed time Boo Boo climbed the steps and entered the rear of the vehicle. Quietly, all of us gathered around the outside of the vehicle to listen. The WO asked Boo Boo "Had he a problem sleeping in the barn? And did he not like sleeping with the rest of us?" Boo Boo nervously tried to explain, but was stopped by the WO who said "Look lad if you are not prepared to sleep over there, you can come here". A sharp intake of breath! The WO continued "Report back here at 2200hrs with your pyjamas". Another sharp intake of breath! A moments pause, then Boo Boo blurted out "Your one of them!"

"One of what?" replied the WO. "You know, One of them!" Without a moments hesitation there was a skurry of boots and Boo Boo was seen leaving the vehicle in treble time, his feet never touched the ladder. It wasn't until he had landed on the ground that he was aware of the roars of laughter from all who had witnessed it. He'd been wound up.

Resolution

In the Army, we had a Warrant Officer,
Who really was a pig,
For he criticized and bullied us,
in everything we did,
So one day, we decided we'd had enough,
We plotted to take our revenge.
Watching him closely,
we soon discovered his weakness,
For he had a haemorrhoid,
to him it was a pain,
Something that caused him discomfort,
but pleased us all the same.
On his next time to the bathroom,
we changed his ointment,
With a substitute, a tube of gasket sealant,
After the application he never was the same.
The moral of this story is:
To resolve a situation,
Get to the bottom of the problem first!

In the autumn of 1966 I started to have trouble with both my knees and I had to report sick. The Doctor prescribed heat treatment, so I went to the Medical Room for the treatment. I was to sit in front of an Heat lamp with both my knees exposed to the lamp, but, unfortunately the Orderly switched on both the Infra red and ultra violet rays. Within 15 minutes both my knees were 'cooked', and I had to have both my legs covered in calamine lotion. It is not often that you see a soldier wearing blue PT shorts with white legs and boots in the middle of November in Germany. I was subjected to much military humour for at least fourteen days.

During Exercises with the Squadron I was allocated to one of the Sections as their mechanic, and as such I used to act as last vehicle in all their convoys.

In the depth of winter in 1967 I was following my allotted group of vehicles in some very icy and snowy conditions. It was the middle of the night and we came to a valley, which we had to descend on the south side. Our vehicles were spread out about 50yds apart, because of the treacherous conditions, and there were about eight trucks in front of me.

As we started to descend into the valley I could see in the frozen mist that there was a bridge which was illuminated from end to end. And as I was looking down upon it, it had the illusion of a stage viewed from the upper circle of a theatre. The closer I got to the bridge the more visible it became, although still blanketed in a haze of frost. The lead truck entered the bridge and was nearly halfway across it when it started to slew sideways. Skidding on the icy roadway, the truck mounted the pavement, and hit the side railings of the bridge, breaking them loose from their mountings. The front wheels of the truck then dropped over the parapet of the bridge and stopped, hanging there supported by the railings. Below were the freezing waters of a fast flowing river. By now the second truck was on the bridge and seeing what had happened to the first truck, the second driver tried to take evasive action. But in doing so, the second truck now hit the back end of the first truck, knocking it further over the parapet. Desperately, the driver of the first truck was clambering out of the top of his cab and attempting to claw up the canopy to the rear of his truck. The third truck now entered the bridge, and again tried to take evasive action, but ended up sliding to the left of the second truck and slowly coming to a halt, narrowly missing both the previous trucks. The fourth truck stopped just before the bridge.

From my viewpoint above the bridge, the whole incident had appeared as though it were in slow motion and as gracefully as a Swan Lake Ballet. Fortunately no-one was hurt. But the bridge had to remain closed until all the vehicles involved could be recovered and removed from the bridge which was many hours later.

My family accommodation on this posting was in a group of flats at Hubbelrath, there were German Civilians in neighbouring blocks and American Servicemen at the end of ours. We lived on the middle floor.

In Germany at this time we used to carry out an Exercise that was called 'Quick Train', this was basically an emergency evacuation by the Unit with all vehicles and equipment within two hours of the order being given. Some times this Order came in the middle of the night, which necessitated all married personnel to be roused from their married quarters, usually with a lot of noise, shouting, vehicle doors slamming etc which also disturbed the German residents, much to their annoyance.

In December 1967 I was told that I had been allocated a place on my Regimental Proficiency Course Class 1, starting just after Christmas at Depot REME. So I requested leave for Christmas with my family to visit my parents in London.

Arriving in the UK, I was struck down ill for about four weeks, with ulcers and I rapidly lost a lot of weight. Fortunately I was at my parent's house and my wife was able to look after me, but it meant that I lost my place on the RPC course. When I was classed fit by the Doctor I had to report to my Depot, before returning to Germany. During my illness one of my children had acquired a mouse, which he kept in a bird cage, in the back of the car. On my drive to the Arborfield Depot I passed through Windsor, and all the traffic was stopped for the Changing of the Guards. It was then that I spotted the mouse on the top of my kit in the rear of the car, so I jumped out and opened the back door and was able to capture said mouse. But, as I turned to close the door, a lady in a sports car behind me, on seeing the mouse screamed and fainted. I quickly got back into my car and drove off in the commotion.

The mouse later reappeared whilst we were travelling on the Belgium autobahn back to Dusseldorf, up my trouser leg! Only to disappear again.

Once back at the flats at Hubbelrath I fully unloaded the car only to find in the spare wheel was a nest of twelve baby mice. I tried to take them to a pet shop, with no joy, so my children pleaded that we should keep them, in the cage. Joke! Inevitably they got out and disappeared again. At night they could be heard moving about in the panelling of the flats. It was a good thing that we were relocated to a Married Quarter on the outskirts of Dusseldorf not long after.

It was lovely to have a house, and a cellar, with it's own boiler room, which provided the hot water and heating. The children had a small enclosed garden, with flower beds, and I took a pride in caring for the flowers. Till one day I returned home and on checking the flowers found that all the heads had been stuck back on, and were now falling off. My wonderful children had had a flower picking day, and my Wife had tried to repair the damage by sticking the heads back on.

In 1968 the new Ministry of Defence (MOD) had decided upon a further re-organisation of the Army, and 5 Brigade (BDE), of which 17 Sqn was part was to be withdrawn to the UK. We were to be rebased at Deverill Barracks, Ripon, in Yorkshire. The Unit packed up and we all moved to Ripon.

Deverill Barracks was still one of the old Spider type Barracks, situated around a Regimental Square, at the lower end was situated the REME Workshop and Vehicle Parks. A majority of the Married Quarters were located further down the slope of the hill, below the Workshop and Barracks.

On the opposite side of the access road to Deverill was the more permanent Claro Barracks occupied by the Royal Engineers, this was a more modern brick built camp.

Chapter Six
(Return to the UK 1968 – 70)

Our Married Quarter in Ripon was amongst the houses of the Estate below the camp, and there was a passage way next to our house which served as a short cut between the rest of the Estate and the Barracks.

In those days our milk was delivered daily to our doorstep at around 4am each day. The bottles were glass with wax disc inserts in the top to seal them.

I normally rose at 6am and took in the milk shortly afterwards. That is, until one morning our milk was missing from the doorstep. The same thing happened the next morning as well. So someone who was passing our house was taking our milk, so I decided to do something about it. That day I cleaned out an old milk bottle and into it I poured white paint and swirled it around until all the inside was covered. I poured out the surplus paint and left the bottle to dry. Next, I carefully saved one of the wax tops from another bottle. Once the paint was dry, I poured a strong mixture of cooking oil and salt water into the painted bottle. I then gingerly fitted the wax disc into the bottle neck. The bottle now had the appearance of a full bottle of milk.

The following morning I rose as soon as the day's milk was delivered, and I substituted the real milk bottle with my 'prepared' one. As suspected this bottle disappeared from my doorstep.

When I went to work later at 8am, I saw the smashed milk bottle outside the Barrack gates. Someone didn't like my delivery, and left my milk alone in future!

A major event that did happen during our time in Ripon was that there was an horrendous thunderstorm, and rain that was falling onto the regimental square in Deverill, started to shed it's way down off the square through the Workshop and Vehicle Compound and continued further down the hill into the married quarters, where it rose rapidly to about two foot deep. This deluge flooded the streets and the houses of the quarters, so much so that water was seeping into the houses and out the back doors.

Unfortunately, as the water had flowed through the workshop and vehicle compound it had accumulated any areas of oil in its way. This mixture then flooded down through the surface drains and had exited through manhole covers and drains in the streets below, leaving a shining film wherever it flowed. The clean up operation lasted weeks after the water had subsided.

July 1968 I was promoted to Corporal and given the responsibility of running the Unit Battery Charging Bay. All the unit vehicles had lead acid type batteries, and they were in need of constant attention, and recharging. The battery charging bay was a building on its own, and was equipped with two large Charging Machines, large Carboids of Distilled Water and Electrolyte, an Acid Bath and a fresh water tub, numerous connecting cables and a fan ventilation system. I was provided with a face mask, rubber protective clothing and gloves.

My daily routine was to reconnect any batteries to the chargers, and then slowly increase the charging rate up to the required amount for the number of batteries needing charging. After that it was a case of supervision of the process until the batteries were fully charged. To be expected, some batteries that were presented for charging were defective, and I had heavy duty testing equipment to establish any problems. Occasionally I would have to empty a battery into the acid bath, in order to wash out any sediment between the cells and then refill the battery with fresh electrolyte, after which I then had to recharge the battery.

At the height of summer, it was the fumes in the bay that were the worst, hence the ventilation system. It was an interesting period of work for me.

As part of the unit's commitment to 5BDE, and it's supporting roll to NATO, the Unit was required to return each year for a period of ten weeks to participate in Exercises with Units still based in Germany.

In September of 1968 the unit prepared to embark at Felixstowe for Dunkerque. The ships that were used were the Royal Fleet Auxiliary's ships Sir Tristram and Sir Gallahad (sadly, both later lost in the Falkland's conflict) 5 BDE as a whole was over 4000 vehicles, and pieces of mobile equipment, which necessitated long convoys on the Continent's Autobahns, and had to be controlled by both Military and Civilian Police, of all countries involved. This led to an amusing incident when we set off from the harbour in Dunkerque, where the Civil Police were trying to prevent civilian vehicles from getting mixed into the convoy. At one road junction , a civilian in his car, obviously impatient had decided he didn't want to wait, with the result that a Belgium motorcycle Policemen rode along side his car, took out his truncheon and was repeatedly hitting the roof of the said car.

One shipload of about 100 vehicles when in convoy on the Autobahn stretched for about six miles. Ultimately the convoys reached from Dunkerque through Belgium and Holland into Germany.

It was a two day journey to the Training area of Lunneberg Heath, where we set up temporary bases before commencing the Exercises.

One of the more tedious tasks whilst on Exercises is to be detailed for Sentry Duty. For it meant that for about two hours you were expected to conceal yourself at a point on the perimeter and to remain motionless, which in winter time in Germany was uncomfortable and virtually impossible, whilst located in some remote woods.

But my turn came, and having been given the Passwords I was duly dispatched to my post, a narrow track with a ditch running alongside it. Being on the track was too obvious, so I stepped down into the dry ditch, where I could better conceal myself, and so I watched and waited.

In due course, I could hear talking and saw movement coming towards me on the track. I recognised them in the dim light, it was a group of my own unit's Junior Officers. Their intention was to 'test' that each sentry was alert and could 'challenge' them properly. Unfortunately, they seemed to consider themselves immune from any action, because they made no attempt to approach quietly.

I waited, and at 10 yards, I gave them the 'challenge' to which I expected the correct reply. But, No, they stopped in a small group, and stood talking amongst themselves. I could hear them clearly saying "Where is he? Can anybody see where the Sentry is?".

Whilst they were deliberating, I took the opportunity to silently approach them by moving towards them in the ditch, until I was within a yard of them, looking up at them. They were still talking amongst themselves. I couldn't control myself any longer, so with great delight I shouted "BANG" at them. On mass they all leapt into the air. When they landed I calmly said "Your all dead". Having realized what had happened, and trying to save face, one subaltern spluttered out "Well Done, jolly well done". They quickly retreated.

Lunneberg is a massive training area of heath land larger than Salisbury Plain, it had allocated parking areas and some buildings. Because we were situated there for so long we had a Mobile Bath & Laundry Unit (MBLU) visit us with it's large tents for showers and washing facilities, but other facilities were a bit more primitive:

Ring of Fire

In the Army camp, was a little row,
Where soldiers, who were desperate,
could sit and have a go,
Of toilet cubicles, but nothing refined,
Just a wooden seat, with a hole for their behind,
Because there in the open, no wall to confine,
To keep out pests, from vermin it did suffer,
Running back and forth, in the communal gutter.
The instruction, it was given, to clear the lot out,
Up came a soldier, who poured with a spout,
Petrol in the first one, and let it flow within,
But, unknown to him, another soldier had entered in,
On the end seat, with his trousers around his boots,
Hoping for a quiet drag, upon his charoot,
He struck up his lighter, and all went with a bang,
Surprised, he got more than his desire,
For screaming loudly, he had a ring of fire!

In the spring of 1969, back in Ripon, I was on duty as the Recovery Mechanic for the unit and I was called out to attend an accident on one of the country lanes not far from Ripon. A Bedford had left the road and gone through a railed fence and come to a halt in a small wood. So with the Leyland Recovery vehicle I set off to recover this Bedford.

The country lane was narrow, on a bend and on the brow of a small hill. Why the Bedford had left the road I don't recall. But it had mounted a grass verge at the brow of the hill crashed through a metal fence and ended up about 20 feet from the lane.

Using the equipment on the Leyland it should have been a fairly straight forward retrieval. Realising that to try and operate the Crane etc, whilst the Leyland was static on the lane was not safe, so I chose to mount the grass verge parallel to the fence. I used an hacksaw to cut the 15 foot section of damaged fence free, I then needed to lift it clear, for me to gain access to the Bedford. Slewing the crane sideways I connected it to the damaged fence, and started to lift it up, not realising that the foundations for the fence were set in blocks of concrete, which when free of the ground left holes in the soil into which the Leyland slipped sidewise. The Leyland was now stuck itself in the empty holes. Embrassement, I had to phone my unit and report my predicament. I was told to stay with the vehicle over night and help would come in the morning. Help did come in the morning, with it's crowd of onlookers, and critics. The lane had to be fully closed whilst another Leyland recovered both my vehicle and the Bedford.

In the UK 17 Sqn RCT as a unit consisted of Sections of different categories of transport. One Section was Bedford General Service 4 ton trucks, the second Section was of !0 ton trucks , and then the third Section was now re-equipped with Scammel Constructor Tractors and 30 ton trailers.

It was to the third Section that I was now attached to as their mechanic.

1969 was the year when matters in Northern Ireland started to take a turn for the worse, and the Government decided to start increasing the military presence there. This involved the movement of a lot of heavy equipment and vehicles as well as manpower.

The Scammels were now allocated with the task of travelling to various units within the UK and collecting, and transporting items to the docks at Liverpool, for onward transportation to Northern Ireland.

Bulford, Chatham, Kirton Lindsey were a few of the places where we transported mostly vehicles and engineer equipment from. Our usual routine was to leave Ripon late on Sunday night and travel to which unit required our assistance.

In all there were 10 of these Scammels and trailers, and most of them had come into Army Service in 1939 – 40, their top speed was only 20 mph (with the wind behind them). All were equipped with Gardiner 6 cylinder petrol engines, but their steering was air operated, and they made a fearful row when they were moving. Each Tractor unit had to supplied with additional metal blocks of ballast, to enable them to have enough traction under load, so they weighed about 25 tonnes each fully fitted.
The trailers were British Made trailers of eight wheels, mounted in four pairs. To load a trailer the rear two pairs of wheels had to be removed, a ramp fitted to enable vehicles to be driven onto them. Then the wheel units had to be refitted for the road. Sometimes, depending whether they were carrying an armoured vehicle, the total tonnage for the tractor and loaded

trailer was in excess of 60 tonne, and a total length of about 80 feet.

Our first trip to Liverpool was an experience, on arrival at the City we were directed to an area of waste ground on the outskirts, to await further instructions to proceed to the Docks. Parking all the Scammels with their respective loads, and Escort Vehicles, naturally drew a lot of local interest. Especially amongst younger children and teenagers. It was the first time I had ever seen young children in this country walking about bare footed, because a majority of them didn't wear any footwear.

Some of the more enterprising youngsters approached our drivers and offered to guard our vehicles for us for a couple of shillings, they said just in case our windscreens got smashed. The result was that we ourselves had to stand guard on the parked vehicles.
Some of these collection journeys lasted a whole week, leaving Ripon on Sunday night, with two days to reach our collection point, then a day to load up, and then a further two days to reach Liverpool, offload and then maybe two days returning to Ripon.

Many of our journeys involved driving through major towns or Cities, and involved careful co-operation with local authorities. At these times all the vehicles had to drive 'nose to tail', to form a continuous convoy of vehicles, and with the assistance of local Police and Escorts we managed to travel without incident.

On one move we had to drive around the North Circular Road of London. It was usual practice for each convoy to be accompanied by a lead vehicle, with a 'wide load' warning sign, and a tail vehicle with a similar sign displayed on its rear. I was travelling in the rear vehicle, which was a left hand drive and I was sat on the offside seat.

As the convoy of vehicles made its way around the North Circular we did so nose to tail and weaving about the road like a long snake to avoid obstacles. At one junction the two lane road we were on changed to a single lane, and the vehicles manoeuvred for the change to the centre of the road. Up to this point we had managed to keep following cars from overtaking us and getting into the convoy, but one driver could not wait any longer and he overtook the tail vehicle, ignoring my signals for him not to do so. The driver then started to overtake the last of the transporter trailers and got almost as far as the tractor unit, before the tractor manoeuvred to the right to line up for the single road. At this point there was a keep left island in the centre of the road, and the car screeched to a halt, unable to proceed any further. The Transporter, however was still manoeuvring to the right and as it did so, its trailer with its heavy duty latching eyes sticking out from its side started to pass the now halted car. As the trailer passed the car each latching eye tore into the nearside bodywork of the car opening it up like a tin can from rear to front. Because the car was in the transporter driver's blind spot, the car was 'unseen' and because of the noise of the ancient transporter's engines any horn was unheard, the affect of 'opening' the car was also unfelt because of the transporter's power.

Later when the convoy was stopped, and the irate car driver tried to complain to the police, because I had witnessed this incident I had to explain that it was the inpatients of the driver and his ignoring all signs to stop him that had led to the incident.

Another trip took us to Salisbury and our route took us around Oxford on the by-pass. The Scammels were nearly thirty years old and as a result were in constant need of attention and repair. In the distance I could see one of our tractors pulled into the side of the road and smoke was belching from underneath it. When I arrived the driver was stood with an empty fire extinguisher having discharged its contents under the vehicle. It become clear that one of the rubber mounted bearings that held the drive shafts had seized up and with the friction had caught fire. My task therefore was to disconnect this bearing and isolate it, so under the vehicle I went with my tools, reappearing not long afterwards having completed the task.

The fire extinguisher that the driver had used was a foam one, and as I came out from under the vehicle I was covered from head to foot in this foam. Just as a family car was slowly passing by and a curious little boy having stuck his head out of the car window, saw me and said to his dad –" Look Dad, a snowman!"

Our last trip was to Kirton Lindsey from the south and we had been directed to drive through the City of

Lincoln, our routes were always specified by the MOD. This time the convoy consisted of just eight Scammel combinations, plus escort vehicles. On crossing the Pelham Bridge in Lincoln we were stopped by the Police, and told that we could not travel up the steep Lindum Hill. So we waited for authority to be redirected. The result was chaos for Lincoln, because it took the convoy over two hours to manoeuvre through the tight streets of the City before ascending the lesser climb of Yarborough Hill.

Having now served for ten years I was beginning to think about my career prospects, I still had not gained all my qualifications for further promotion, and time was passing me by. I still needed to pass my RPC class 1 course of about six weeks, and my Trade Class 1 Mechanic's course of up to nine months at SEME Bordon. If, I were selected for Artificer Training (with possible promotion up to Warrant Officer Class 1 rank) I would then have to return to SEME for a further course lasting eighteen months. I considered this was a lot of time still to be spent in Training Units, most of which time would be at SEME Bordon. Should I not be selected for Artificer Training, I would remain as an Artisan, with eventual promotion to Sergeant or maximum Staff Sergeant for my 22 years. By now I was beginning to tire of being a mechanic. My prospects to be an Artificer were fading.

Before I could make up my mind, I was posted in February 1970 back to BAOR, to 23 Amphibious Engineer Squadron Workshop REME, based at Hameln, on the Weser.

Chapter Seven
(BAOR 1970 – 76)

23 Squadron Royal Engineers, was a unique unit in the British Army, not just because it was amphibious, but because it had German manufactured vehicles. This German equipment was Amphibious Ferry and Bridging vehicles, a majority of which were still under warranty with the manufacturers Eisenwerkkaiserslautern (EWK) and Klocknerhumboltdeutsch (KHD).

Because of the warranty it meant that the manufacturers used to send mechanics and engineers to the unit to carrying out any work that was required. This was ideal for our mechanics because it meant that they could work alongside the Germans and learn more about the equipment.

When I first arrived at the unit I was put onto an Introduction Course to learn about the vehicles, now called M2Bs. Having completed the introduction I started work on the workshop floor. Because I had previously served in Germany, I had learnt and could speak the language, it was here that this ability was put to use by the workshop because interpreters were needed to work with the Germans. From the workshop floor I progressed to the Workshop Office, where I wrote out Job Sheets as required in both English and German languages. I also completed information sheets on all work carried out, that was then sent to the UK for placing on the Army Computer Data Base.

Unknowingly whilst doing all this translation I was also learning German Technical Language, where words could reach unbelievable lengths:

For example:

Auspuffkrummerditchtung = exhaust manifold gasket

Sechtsgangautomatischergetreibe = six speed automatic gearbox.

In May 1970, the Squadron was expanded into 28 Amphibious Engineer Regiment, and the Workshop increased in size as well.

Members of the Workshop were now REME, Royal Engineers, RAOC, and the Germans on occasions, over 100 personnel in all.

The OC of the Workshop and admin staff were all REME, but we had a Royal Engineer Ssgt who was designated as our Workshop Sgt Major (WSM). I worked in the Workshop Office for about a year, and was happy to do so, when our Admin Chief Clerk had to go on Compassionate leave to the UK.

The Chief was the only Clerical member of the unit, and to my surprise he asked me to stand in for him as temporary admin staff. So I moved to his office for the duration. I found the hours long and at times difficult because admin is totally different to technical, but I persevered.

When the Chief returned he asked me to stay and work in his office, as the Establishment for the Unit was one Sgt Clerk (himself) and a Corporal Clerk (clerical). We discussed my adopting the role of a Dual Tradesman, because officially I was still classed as a Mechanic, and becoming a qualified Clerk as well. My Records office was asked to approve this action, and they did on the condition that I take the necessary Clerical Trade Test qualifications to meet the role of Corporal Clerk, and then I could fill the vacancy in the Establishment.

I took lessons from the Chief, taught myself to type, and by February 1972, I was classed as Corporal Clerk Class 2, then my Records office granted me the Dual Trade status.

Having served two years in the unit as a Mechanic, my Records Office now reposted me to the unit as the Corporal Clerk for a further two years. It was during this period that I learnt the anomalies of the different Corps in the unit. Mainly the individual Record Office Instructions for each Corps. These Instructions dealt with all the different matters that were peculiar to that particular Corps, especially the REME and Royal Engineers, and this proved to be useful knowledge to me when I was later posted to a Royal Engineer unit in 1978.

Even though I was now employed as a Cpl Clerk due to the anomalies of the Pay Structure, and the difference in the Trade Pay Scales, I continued to receive the pay of a Corporal Class 2 Mechanic (because it is a higher Trade Pay Scale than that of a Clerk). This was only going to change, by increase when I was promoted to Sgt Clerk, when the rank increased the amount.

During these four years my family had now moved from a Married Quarter in Hannover, to a village near Hameln called Tundern, and then from there to a Flat in another village named Hastenbeck. It was in this flat that we started to experience the problems of bigger families, we now had five young children. We lived below a flat of older children, who when their parents were out would resort to all sorts of tricks, from having parties or playing loud music, vomiting out of their windows.

With the expansion of the Squadron to becoming a Regiment, a new compound was built on the outskirts of Hameln to accommodate all the M2Bs and a new Workshop to service them, it was called Gundolph Park,

My four years at Hameln now up, I was posted to 5 Field Workshop REME near Soest, as a Corporal Clerk. Here, I met up with one of my previous Chief Clerks from Hameln. 5 Fd Wksp was solely a REME Workshop. Here, I was employed as the Orderly Room Corporal, supervising four junior Clerks but under the Chief who was now a Warrant Officer. The unit was established for a Ssgt Clerk to supervise the Orderly Room but he didn't arrive for a few months, which left me fulfilling the role. I was now getting excellent Annual Reports with recommendation for promotion to Sgt, but only after I had passed my Class one Clerical exam, which I completed in March 1973.

Soest was a town that we knew from our posting to Lippstadt in 1963, when the Canadians were based there and had occupied the Married Quarters. We thought it a depressing place, and when we were allocated a Married quarter in Soest itself, my family did not like it. Daily travel for the children to school was by bus all the way to Hamm. The Quarters themselves were all flats, and again we experienced problems with older families. My wife and I were beginning to get disenchanted with this move and we decided, for the whole families' sake for her to move back to Scotland. So in November 1974 my family moved to Aberdeen, but because of accommodation problems there, we had to ask SSAFA and Family Welfare for assistance and a Married Quarter was provided in Dundee. Meanwhile, I remained in Soest and moved into the barracks.

Each Wednesday afternoon in the unit it was Sports Time, and it was on one of these days that all the Clerks went to a stable near to the Moehnesee, to hire horses for an experience. At the stable the owner was only too pleased, and he produced a number of horses and saddles, and in due course the clerks all set off down the country lane, with the knowledge that the horses knew where they we going. My horse was the last to be saddled and it was the biggest of the group, as soon as I was sat in the saddle the horse set off at a trot to catch the group up. The horse continued past the group and took up the lead, and we all rode peacefully down the lane until we reached an open gateway where my horse turned into the field, which was ploughed, and as if by signal all the horses set off across this field in what felt like a gallop. At the last moment before reaching the far side, my horse decided to come to a sudden halt, me, not expecting this, ended up flying over the horses head and landing in the ploughed field with my legs wide open and scooping up soil as I came to a halt. Remounting the horse we proceeded back to the stables. It was only then that the owner told me that my horse was the leader, and always played this trick on the unwary.

Leaving the stables the Clerks now wanted to go ice skating. Again, I had never skated in my life so I was hanging onto the rail all the way around the arena, Of course I lost my balance and fell numerous times upon the ice, to everybody's amusement. Except the owner of the ice rink, because every time I fell I left a sample of soil from the field.

When my family had first moved to Soest I had purchased a ford transit mini bus. With my family now in Scotland I started to provide transport for various events for the unit, and at some weekends I would transport furniture and possessions for families moving back to the UK. I also used this bus in many forms (by re-arranging the seats) to do various transport tasks unofficially, for the unit.

It was to my surprise one day that the Chief Clerk, called me into his office and introduced me to a civilian, whom I recognised as the camp Cinema Manager, he was a civilian, but employed by the forces (SKC – Services Kinema Corporation). It was explained to me that the manager's wife had recently died, and that there were problems with trying to arrange the funeral of the lady.

Being located in Western Germany, and attached to the occupying forces, the funeral could not be carried out without a great deal of paperwork with the German civilian authorities, as the deceased held dual nationality, being born in France and married to an Englishman. However, a funeral could be arranged under Forces authority, but this status did not entitle the use of military vehicles, hence I was asked to assist with my bus. Naturally, I agreed, and I was given all the necessary details of the church service, size of coffin and the place of burial, but one small problem arose straight away, in that it was traditional to drape the coffin in the national flag of the deceased. In the unit we had a suitable Union Jack, but not a French Tricolour. Fortunately, I had seen various flagpoles outside the town supermarket, flying international flags, so I visited the store, and the staff were kind enough to loan me a tricolour. The Union Jack and the Tricolour were joined together and later draped over the coffin.

In my bus, I temporarily removed two of the larger seats assemblies on the right hand side, leaving just two single seats, one behind the other, along the left side of the vehicle. I retained the dual seat at the front of the vehicle next to the driver for any other passengers. Black ribbon was given to me to decorate the exterior of the vehicle with bows. My passengers were to be, the Admin Officer (a friend of the manager), the Chief Clerk (as representative of the unit and organiser of the burial party), the two rear single seats were occupied by soldiers of the burial party. The manager travelled in another car driven by a friend with a further two soldiers of the burial party. There weren't any other relatives to attend.

On the day of the funeral, the weather was a fine hot sunny day. The church service was held in the unit church with only a few people in attendance. After the service the coffin was carried with due solemnity and placed onto a hidden plinth into the rear of my bus. All of the flowers were placed upon the top of the coffin. The escorting soldiers occupied the two side seats next to the deceased. The Officer and Chief Clerk sat on the front seats next to me.

The burial was to be in the Forces Cemetery at Rheindahlen, approximately 100 miles away, and so we set off, driving through the camp to the main gates at walking pace. The easiest way to get to Rheindahlen was to use the autobahn, which was less than two miles from the camp, and I drove this distance at a sedate 25mph. I turned onto the autobahn and continued at the same speed, however, within a few moments the car with the manager, who had been following the bus, overtook us and he shouted through the car window for us to follow them. Which I duly did, at 60mph!

The autobahn was busy with other traffic and it wasn't long before we were being overtaken by coaches of Germans, who upon seeing the black ribbons on the exterior of the bus, became 'curious' – all of the Germans were looking down from there seats into my bus as there coaches slowly overtook the cortege.

From the German's perspective they all saw a coffin with flowers, and two soldiers in attendance, sat with their heads respectively bowed, both the soldiers appeared to be weeping. On the front seat of bus the Officer and Chief were both waving their arms about, and opening their mouths as though they were wailing. A strange state of affairs, plus travelling at 60pmh – I can only guess what the Germans were thinking?

But, in reality, because of the hot day, the soldiers in the rear of the bus were suffering from the excessive use by the Undertakers of the embalming solution, and the pungent strong smell was making everyone's' eyes water, especially those sat next to the coffin.

The day of the funeral was also the day when the English cricket team was playing in the Test Match, and the Officer and Chief were both avid supporters, which is why they had switched on the vehicle radio to hear the match. So, naturally, when England scored they raised their arms in adulation and vocally expressed at key moments. This continued all the way along the autobahn.

Off the autobahn and approaching Rheindahlen, the car with the manager pulled into a lay-by, and I followed suit. The manager stepped out of the car and came and spoke to the Officer. Having travelled there at such speed we were now ahead of the schedule for the burial ceremony, The manager said that he was thirsty and fancied a drink so he suggested that we all went to the local NAAFI. When asked respectfully about leaving the coffin, the manager said that it would be alright to leave her in the car park!

Whilst in the NAAFI the two escort soldiers who had travelled in the bus, drew attention to themselves because they were continually sneezing because of the odour from the coffin.

Duly refreshed and at the appointed time we travelled to the cemetery, where another Minister was waiting. The burial party 'fell in' and carried the coffin to the grave, where the Minister conducted a brief ceremony accompanied by the sneezing of the two escorts. Calamity was narrowly averted when the coffin was being lowered, because of the sneezing, the two escorts nearly lost control of the sashes supporting the coffin, the Chief was quick to step forward and take hold, to the amazement of the Minister, who himself nearly slipped and fell into the grave. The Minister landed rather unceremoniously on his backside. After the burial, all but the manager withdrew a discrete distance to allow him a few last moments with his wife.

Having said his goodbyes the manager told us that he needed another drink and so we all retired to the NAAFI, again. Although the manager was a quiet man, he did explain to us all that his wife had been ill for some time now, we could see how the strain of caring for his wife had affected him.

We set off on the return journey to camp, to the never ending accompaniment of the sneezing, cricket and again at 60pmh!

In barracks I had befriended an NCO who introduced me to the The Royal Antideluvian Order of Buffalos (RAOB) and I joined the organisation in March 1975.

As the Orderly Room Corporal I was given the task of preparing the four wheeled office trailer for an exercise. This involved not only cleaning it, but repainting it in camouflage colours as well. Even with two inch paintbrushes it took myself and some of the clerks all day to finish the task and on returning to the office at about 1600hrs the Chief Clerk said the trailer looked good, but had we painted the roof as well? We hadn't, so I was detailed to finish the task. Reluctantly out I went and by tea time I had finished, the trailer looked pretty good. Days later we set off on the exercise, and it was my Bedford truck that pulled the trailer. Heading for the Autobahn the Chief Clerk and Admin Officer passed us in their free running landrover. Once on the autobahn we settled down to a usual convoy drive, watching all the civilians pass us by laughing at our lack of speed, when into view came an overhead bridge and the figures of the Chief Clerk and Admin Officer could be seen leaning over the rails watching the unit vehicles passing below them. Only then could I smile to myself, because I couldn't later, for on the roof of the trailer I had painted a giant sunflower!

Regardless of my antics, and on gaining all my qualifications and recommendations for promotion, I was promoted To Sgt Clerk and posted as Orderly Room Sergeant to 48 Command Workshop REME, Cyprus in April 1976.

Chapter Eight
(Cyprus 1976 – 78)

I now found myself in a new world, for years I had been the Senior of the Junior NCOs, but now I was the junior of the Senior NCOs. It takes time to acclimatize to this transition, Mess Life, the extra responsibilities etc.

48 Command Workshop REME, had been based in Dhekalia for years, but because of the Turkish invasion of Cyprus in 1974, it was decided to relocate the Workshop to the RAF Base at Akrotiri. It was during this transition period that I arrived to take up post. I had a senior Chief Clerk, but he was located at the Headquarters in Episkopi.

The relocation of the Workshop occupied two of the large Hangars at Akrotiri, alongside the main runway, plus an assortment of smaller builders for the supporting trades. My office complex was adjoining one of the hangars. This complex consisted of the OC, Admin Officer, Workshop Sergeant Major, myself, civilian typist and office runner.

The unit establishment was for about 70 Senior NCOs, who supervised a civilian staff of about 200 Greeks, in all trades, and being a Command Workshop carried out repairs on all types of equipment, and manufacture.

Initially, I nervously settled into the routine of work and Mess life. My family were now able to rejoin me in

Cyprus, and we settled into our married quarter bungalow not far from the Workshop, but within the confines of the RAF Base. My children were now educated at the Service School in Episkopi and travelled there daily by service bus. My wife started to participate in various Wives' activities and was enjoying the relaxed atmosphere and warmth.

My office was classed as a Secure Office with combination locks on both my entrance door and filing cabinets, my windows were all screened. As a hot climate area, our daily work routing was usually to start work about 0700hrs and usually finish about 1300hrs, leaving us with the whole afternoon for recreation. This my children loved because it normally meant a trip to the beach until tea time.

One morning I arrived at work as usual, only to find that all the military staff were dressed for a day's training, I wasn't. Because of a misunderstanding on my part, an argument ensued. I now stormed off, and for some reason locked myself in my office, to which no-one could gain access. Repeatedly, various NCOs came to my door, but I refused to acknowledge them. Without realising it I must have been experiencing another episode similar to the one I had suffered in 1964. I only left the office when all was quiet, and I returned to my married quarter.

Next morning when I went to my office, to find that the door was open and my Chief Clerk from Episkopi was sat in my office waiting for me. He informed me that I was to be 'marched' in front of the OC that morning on a disciplinary matter.

In due course I was brought before my OC, who informed that I was to be placed on a 'Three month's Warning Order' (basically a three months period of probation – in which time I was expected to improve my position or stand the chance of losing my rank and post). This action hit me like a hammer blow, because as far as I recall, a copy of this Order was automatically forwarded to my Records Office, where it was placed in my Service Records, the effect was that it could prevent any further consideration for promotion, certainly for the near future, if not for all time.

Militarily, this was the accepted action to be taken according to current Queen's Regulations, but no consideration was given that I might have suffered a Mental Episode as a consequence of the argument. It also undermined my self confidence, to such a degree that I began to question my abilities, I always tried my best, but was it good enough?

Even now 45 years later, I still find it hard to comprehend how not 6 months earlier I was full of confidence and ambition, and then suddenly to lose it all in one day? My subsequent Confidential Reports commented on various aspects of my abilities to do things, but with hindsight, is it not understandable, given the way I was now feeling after the event? I began to doubt myself, my confidence was gone and with it my ambition. But, at the end of the day I still did my job to the best of my abilities, and I think in spite of everything else this was my saving grace.

But, I was also to suffer the long term effect of loss of self confidence and my ability to do things, the wording on the Order read something like "not up to the standards required of his rank". Which I found hard to believe, when not two years before my Confidential Reports were stating that "as a Cpl I was fulfilling the tasks of a Ssgt, a rank well above my own", and that I was receiving praise and recommendations for my abilities. The Order had a stigma that was to affect the rest of my service. I survived the period, but the remainder of my service in Cyprus was under constant scrutiny.

I know that concerns were expressed for my family because my Chief Clerk visited my Wife in our married quarter whilst I was at work, to enquire if she and the children were okay? But, no thought was given to my state of health. Had there been, I could have been referred to the Hospital at Akrotiri, but I wasn't, only then would it have been revealed that I had suffered a similar event back in 1964, and could have been treated for it. As it was, I didn't receive any treatment, and the next three months for me was an agonising and stressful period, which I could have well done without.

On reflection, why didn't I seek Medical help for myself? Quite simply, you do not realise, and hate to accept that you have a problem, added to which, if you did seek help, it would reveal that you do have a problem and it will be seen as a sign of weakness to others. If Medical intervention was brought in, it would also be seen as questioning the Military Authority at the time. Bearing in mind this happened in 1976, when problems of this sort were in there infancy. It was the later conflicts of the Falklands (1982), The Gulf War (1992) and Afghanistan (2001 – 2021) that mental conditions were truly recognised.

1977 was the year of Our Queen's Silver Jubilee, and to commemorate this occasion a Medal was to be issued to all Services. Having missed the opportunity of the General Service Medal in Aden, I had expectations at last. When the issue of the said Medal came it was a disappointment to us all, because there were not enough Medals distributed. The allocation to our Unit was only two Medals. One was taken by our Colonel based at the Headquarters, and the other Medal was 'raffled' off between all the members of the unit, the result was that the Colonel's Driver was given the Medal?

In later years, more consideration was given to the award of various Jubilee Medals with the result that there was a fairer distribution of said Medals.

In Cyprus, our married quarter was at Akrotiri Airbase, on a small escarpment from which we could view activity on the Airfield about 800yds away.
During my time in Cyprus, two major things occurred: The first was a wild fire that broke out in the shrub land between the married quarters and the airstrip, and threatened the married quarters.

The second event was far more dramatic, shortly before 7am on the 7th December 1977, I was getting ready for going to work. From my married quarter, which was about half a mile north of where I worked I could look from the slightly elevated escarpment which permitted me to see not just the hangers of the airstrip but parts of the runway as well. In those days it was usual to see and hear the American U2 plane, nicknamed the 'black budgie' because of it's colour or 'snoopy' after the large character depicted on its tail taking off and landing at the airstrip. It was strange because in spite the plane's mat black colour and taking off into the clear blue Mediterranean sky, the plane disappeared from view long before the sound of the engines had faded away.
This particular morning I could hear the engines warming up and I moved to my veranda to watch it take off. The pitch of the engines rose and I could see the black shape start to move from left to right along the runway, disappearing momentarily behind the hangers as it progressed. But, something was not right! The pitch of the engines seemed to peak and not increase anymore, and the plane was not rising as it usually did, but kept travelling just clear of the ground past the hangers. It neared the area where the Control Tower was, and I saw a flash, followed by a plume of black smoke, I next heard the 'vump' sound. I immediately realised that something was wrong. I jumped on my office bike and rode down to my office, which was not far from the Control Tower.

The RAF Emergency Team was already in action and I was told not to approach the Control Tower area, which by now was engulfed in black smoke and flames.

Our civilian work force, about 200 Greek Cypriots, had been on the runway side of our hangers awaiting admission to work prior to the plane taking off, and it had passed very close to them.

Cypriots later told me what they had seen, that the plane had started to veer off the runway and towards the hangers where they all had stood, but managed to pass by, before crashing into the base of the Control Tower and Communications Centre where several personnel were on duty. Lives were lost, but lives were saved as well by the quick thinking of others who broke into the far end of the buildings.

It was said afterwards that during the previous weekend the usual pilot had been involved in a road traffic accident, and that on the day it was the relief pilot who flew the aircraft, also connections were made with the significance of it happening on the day it did - Pearl Harbour day.

As a member of the RAOB, I was able to join in the use of their facilities on the island. There was a Clubhouse just outside the perimeter of the Base and it was used each day by members and their families, many a happy BBQ was had there, social events were also held, with numerous parties and events for the children. One contribution the RAOB, as an organisation made was to raise money by various means for underprivileged children in the UK to be flown to Cyprus and given a short holiday with our families. My family decided to complete a Fund Raising event by our five sons running a relay the 15 miles from Akrotiri to Episkopi, which they did and raised over 250 Cypriot Pounds, the price of one airfare for a child.

During periods of recreation I attended a National Small-bore & Pistol Coach Course, in which I qualified as an Instructor on 9mm Pistol and Small-bore Weapons.

I did have one moment of glory in Cyprus, in that I was awarded and presented with my Long Service & Good Conduct Medal on completion of 18 years service. But, even this event was marred for me, because less than three weeks after I had been awarded said Medal, the MOD changed the qualifying period for this Medal from 18 years reduced to 15 years, with a Bar to given for a further 7 years Service. Still, I had one Medal at least.

It was not unusual, that having completed a two year tour as a Sgt Chief Clerk to be promoted to Ssgt on the next posting. This obviously did not happen to me, and on completion of my tour, in April 1978, I was notified of a posting to the UK, ironically, again to Ripon, but this time to the other side of the road to 38 Engineer Regiment Workshop REME, as a Sgt Chief Clerk, here my previous knowledge of the different Corps Instructions was to stand me in good stead. I now still had three and a half years to serve before my demob on completing my 22 years engagement.

Chapter Nine
(Posting to UK 1978 – 81)

Again at Ripon, our Married Quarter this time was in the centre of the Estate below the camp that I have previously mentioned. The quarter was small, damp and depressing. Arriving back in the UK in April direct from the warmth of Cyprus was a cold shock, for we only had our warm weather clothing. When our MFO boxes were delivered from storage in Dundee, with all our possessions and clothing they were found to be damaged by poor storage, and little could be salvaged from the boxes, including the much needed clothing. Our return to the UK was a sole destroying experience.

I have said that the Warning Order issued in Cyprus felt like it had a stigma, because on arrival at Ripon and reporting for duty, I had the distinct feeling that the knowledge of this Order was known. Added to this I met again a Sgt Instructor from Hameln, not an impressive reunion.

38 Engineer Regiment, Royal Engineers, was a multi role unit, consisting of various Squadrons that were deployed abroad at various times to carry out engineering tasks. The REME Workshop supported the Regiment and maintained it's numerous pieces of Engineering equipment.

My expectations were to be able to settle into this unit with a fresh start, but I felt that there was an ‘atmosphere’ towards me. Initially, I was the only clerical member, but a Craftsman Clerk straight from training was later posted to us.

I had a strange feeling that I was under scrutiny, especially from my superiors, namely my OC and the Artificer Sergeant Major. Feeling as I did from Cyprus, I felt vulnerable, and unfortunately anyone who displays any sense of vulnerability is soon ‘picked on’ for that weakness, or so it seems.

So for the first year back in the UK I kept my head down and did my job, with little incident, there were some difficulties, but I thought I had overcome them.

1979 I still had two years to serve, and I became eligible to start my Resettlement Programme, where I could apply for Courses and Qualifications that could enhance my prospects for Civil Employment. An important stage in my life was coming, mainly to be a civilian, so my priorities started to gradually change, whilst still trying to maintain my current position.

This started to cause some friction between myself and my seniors, basically, because any absence of mine from the Workshop would leave the clerical posts understaffed, understandably. Some courses were only a week long others were four weeks, and I was made to feel that I was neglecting my work in favour of my future interests. But, how else could I prepare myself for demob? But, my priorities were beginning to change, I had to consider my future life as a civilian, the result was that I tried to work harder and longer when in camp in order to cover my periods of absence. In addition to this I was expected to show some participation in the Regiment, which I did by Qualifying as a Range Officer, which added to my NSRA Instructor qualification permitted me to supervise the Indoor Ranges for the use of .22 weapons for target shooting, which was held every Thursday evening for any member of the Unit and members of their families over the age of 16 years. It was always well attended.

During 1979 myself and the Unit Armourer represented the Regiment at Bisley in the Annual Army Shooting Competition, with little success.

Fishing was fast becoming a growing sport within the Army, so I founded the Regimental Fishing Club, which again included families of the unit. We held many competitions and it was a successful Club.

As mentioned before Wednesday afternoons are usually used for sports events, here I introduced Sea Fishing to the Unit. I used to book a fishing boat based at Filey, and we had fishing trips off Flamborough Head, the only problem here was that we needed the whole day. So it became a monthly event for up to ten personnel, even the Commanding Officer of the Regiment came on one trip and had a successful days fishing, taking a variety of fish home for his tea. Next day on my desk was a letter of appreciation from the CO.

Having been in the Married Quarter for a year, and with only two years to demob, with the aid of the Resettlement Scheme I was able to apply for an advance grant which enabled my wife and I to start a mortgage for our future family home. We chose Lincoln, basically for economical reasons. November 1979, my family vacated the Married Quarter and moved to Lincoln. A major part of the transition to civilian life had begun. This now meant that I would have to move into Barracks and the Sgts' Mess. But I was fortunate that the Mess was full, and the overspill accommodation was in a Spider over in the old Deverill Barracks across the road. I jumped at the chance as it meant that I would not be living 'over the shop' in Claro, and would have more privacy.

The regimental square of the desolate Deverill Barracks used to be utilized occasionally by the Yorkshire Constabulary for riot training. They arrived by the bus load with all their riot gear, which they donned and then lined up on the square to carry out their training. One afternoon as I was leaving early for home the Police were in mid training, advancing and making their noises in full gear with shields at the ready. Seeing my opportunity, whilst I was in motor cycle gear and helmet, I took hold of a nearby dustbin lid and stepped onto my side of the square. I stood there alone facing this wall of Police advancing, I shouted a challenge "Come on, I'll take the lot of you on". To which they responded with laughter. Afterwards, they jeered to me in humour as I rode out of the Barracks.

When my Clerk arrived his work place was in the ASM's office, where repeatedly the ASM gave my Clerk work to do, which interfered with the work which I allocated to him. It came to a head and both the ASM and I had a disagreement, but the point was made that the Clerk was my Admin Staff, and any work that the ASM needed doing had to be given to me and I would arranged for its completion.

With my family now in Lincoln I used to commute by Motorcycle every Friday evening returning to Ripon for Monday morning. My family were now a lot happier and they settled into a civilian routine of education and work.

My meals were all provided in the Sgts' Mess in Claro, after which I would walk to my room in Deverill. The Mess naturally held functions, from Full Mess Dinners, to Social evenings for wives as well.

One Mess Dinner the RSM in conjunction with the ASM decided to call me forward to the head table to receive a 'gift' which he presented me with in front of all in attendance, it was an attempt to humiliate me, because he gave me a woman's blouse. But, I 'bit the bullet' and retaliated, which the RSM didn't expect. I thanked him for the gift and I asked "If his wife could afford to give it to me, as he didn't want to deprive her of what little she had". The RSM was fuming to say the least.

So, continued a period of humiliation by both my ASM and the RSM at any opportunity, both men of whom I had a personal dislike. I found myself with what seemed extra duties, not just for the Regiment but for the Mess as well?

The problems that I had experienced in 1968 with my knees arose again and I ended up for two weeks in Catterick Hospital after an operation that rendered my right knee incapable. I could walk, slowly, but my right leg I had to drag behind me, so I walked with the aid of a walking stick, until my recovery months later.

But, it didn't prevent me from riding my motorcycle. I was also given two weeks sick leave after discharge from the Hospital, another period of absence from my work. As there was only the OC and myself, it fell to me to perform some other duties, for example Family Welfare for which I had to attend a short Course at Birmingham University, and as part of my Resettlement I managed to attend another short Course of Employment Law at Bristol University. My final two years was becoming extremely busy, one way or another. But, in spite of it all I managed to keep my cool, and did all that I could to satisfy not just myself, but the unit as well. My Confidential Reports were now beginning to be more positive, but, sadly too late for me, and I remained a Sgt until my demob in November 1981. So I never achieved my ambition rank.

The question remains though: Was I a good at my job? That I cannot really answer, I did consider that I did do my job the way I had been taught, and at times I did get great satisfaction from that.

I was contacted by my Records Office one day and asked if I would go and visit the home of a young Craftsman who lived in Leeds, and had been seriously injured in a car crash. Sadly, the young man was now wheelchair bound and no longer fit for service, and my Records Office wanted me to take and complete discharge paperwork with him, which I did one evening. Later I received a letter of thanks from his parents and my Records Office for the assistance that I had given.

I may have had my weaknesses, either in my trade skills or personality, but once aware of them, I always tried to overcome them, out of necessity or for my own satisfaction. When I left Ripon for the final time, it was with the knowledge that I had secured my Pension, had my solitary medal in my pocket and with a great sense of relief.

For the next 15 years I received Annual Recall Books, as a Reservist, but they were never activated for the 1982 Falkland's War, 1992 Gulf War or Northern Ireland. This call to Duty was for our Sons to fulfil in due course.

I often ask myself did I enjoy my Service Career? Here I have mixed feelings. But I did have my moments. Had I not joined up, I would not have met my Wife, which would have been the biggest regret of my life, and together we raised a family to be proud of.

Would I join the Army again? In 1959 there was little choice because of Conscription, and I volunteered because all my other career options had failed, but would still not have stopped me from being Conscripted. So, I chose to volunteer and gain all the financial benefits.

Regrettably, I did not achieve the rank status I had so long hoped for, but for the period I served I was fortunate not to be involved in any conflicts or world issues.

Through my Service I not only learnt new trades, but many others skills as well, which I have been able to apply several times since. I had the opportunity to visit many countries that I would probably have never seen. I travelled not only to West Germany, but, Holland, Belgium, Northern France, Denmark, Norway, Aden, Bahrain, Kuwait, Cyprus, and seen the Mediterranean, Egypt and the Suez Canal. During periods of leave whilst in Europe we, as a family, visited Luxembourg, Bavaria, Austria and Northern Italy.

All of which added to our experiences of life, I have seen people who lived in absolute poverty and others who had riches beyond belief. Myself and our children were able to learn foreign languages, never before considered. In this respect I think that we were fortunate.

The Army I joined in 1959 was not the same Army I left in 1981. The Army was evolving, post 1963 all Servicemen were volunteers and therefore treated as such. Times and attitudes were changing.

Chapter Ten
Service Family Life

So far I have mentioned very little about my married life whilst I was in Service, and the effects that it had upon not just myself, but for my Wife and also our children. At the end of my Service my wife and I had five sons, aged 14 to 19 years old, and I know that they each had different experiences during my service.

In the whole twenty years of married life during my service, I spent an estimated total of seven years separated from my family, this was broken down into periods of Exercises (days to months), periods of separation during postings, attachments, final resettlement, and time spent on Courses.

These periods of my absence did place a lot of extra responsibility and strain upon my wife, especially trying to raise five boys. There were squabbles within the Married Quarters when the men were away, between the families, and it fell to the wives to control it in the absence of the men.

But serving and living abroad can be a wonderful and educating experience for the children, not only the opportunity to learn foreign languages, but to visit many places of interest as well. We had some wonderful holidays in Europe as a whole whilst I was based in Germany.

The Children's Education was another concern, moving on average every two years, meant in most cases a new School on each move. This is bound to be disruptive to the child, especially as their respective years progressed. The Army did have a Boarding School Scheme, where children could be educated in the UK whilst the parents served abroad. The big offset here was the overall expense, the more children the higher the expenses to the family, even with financial aid it was a major outlay beyond my reach. And there was also to be considered the additional periods of separation from the children. Moving on postings every two years, could mean from Germany to the UK or further afield. Here, the children experienced different systems of education, Military to Civilian being the biggest. My family moved from Germany to Scotland, to Cyprus, and then to England. With a mixture of Junior, Secondary and Grammar School systems, this is hard upon any child, because even in England I had the youngest child in Ripon Grammar School, whilst his four siblings were at the Secondary School on the opposite side of the road, and each School discouraged their pupils to mix with the other. Some Civilian Schools had strange, even biased attitudes towards pupils of 'Army' families. Standards of Homework were different, and must have been a nightmare for their mother to deal with.

They say that children follow their father's career, three of our sons did, and joined various units of the Army when they were old enough.

I do regret not being at home with my family, but I had a job to do, and it was this job that kept the family fed and housed. You do eventually adapt to it, but it is still heart wrenching when we had to separate, even for the shortest periods.

There is also the point that with the father being away so often, that the children become more resilient, and independent whilst standing stronger together as a family.

Fortunately the relationship between myself and my Wife, although it did have it's moments, we did survive, and our marriage lasted 53 years until her death in 2014.

Chapter Eleven
Resettlement to Civilian Life

After twenty two years of living a Regimented and supportive lifestyle it is difficult to adjust ones ways to be a Civilian, there is no safety net, you hope that all the qualifications that you have earned and all the skills that you have learnt will be acceptable to any future employer. The Resettlement Scheme offered opportunities, Courses and advice, but it is up to the individual to find his future employment. It could mean endless visits to the Job Centres, answering Job Adverts, and all this hopefully could be done before your final discharge date.

The Army Resettlement Scheme started two years before demob, with Financial Benefits that could help you secure a future home, it seems like a long time, but it passes very quickly. In the end, it all falls upon the individual to find their new future. Serving the final two years is a 'juggling act', on one hand you are trying to do all that you can to secure your future, whilst on the other hand you are trying to maintain your present commitments, and not let standards fall. Personally I didn't find this easy. There were moments of conflict.

Now, at the age of 80 years I am considered a Veteran, I have my memories, my stories and my medal. I meet other Veterans, and together we recall our Service years, banter of years long past.

Summary of Qualifications gained during my Service.

Trade:

1961	Vehicle Mechanic (Electrician) Class 3
1964	Vehicle Mechanic (B – E) Class 2
1972	Clerk REME Class 3 & 2
1973	Clerk REME Class 1
1979	HGV Driver Class 1

Qualifications:

1957 – 1981	Driving License Groups, A, D, E.
1964	Army Certificate of Education Class 1, Maths & English
1965	Army Certificate of Education Class 1, Map Reading.
1971	Army Certificate of Education Class 1, Admin within the Unit.
1971	Awarded Education Proficiency Certificate (Advanced) Class 1.
1977	National Small-bore & Rifle Association (Pistol Coach)
1979	Institute of Supervisory Management AMISM
1981	Member of the Institute of Supervisory Management MISM
1981	Certificate of Professional Competence (National Road Haulage).
1981	Certificate of Professional Competence (International Road Haulage).

Short Courses:

1979	Bristol University, Behaviour at Work (Stress Analysis)
1980	Birmingham University, Family Welfare (welfare problems)
1981	Bristol University, Employment Law (Legislation)

Additional Courses Attended:

1960	Army Certificate of Education Class 2.
1961	Wheeled Armoured Car Trained.
1961	16mm & 35mm Cine Projectionist
1964	Public Relations (Photographer)
1970	M2 Amphibious Bridge Vehicle Trained
1971	German Language Course.
1971	Regimental Proficiency Class 1
1971	Typing (Evening Classes)
1974	Unit Documentation Course
1977	Woodworking (Evening Classes)
1980	St John's Ambulance First Aid Certificate (Evening Classes)
1981	Junior Management Certificate Resettlement

Other books published by this Author:

Bilko's Book of Banter

A collection of humorous poems, and different Poetic views of life, dedicated to his Wife.
ISBN 9781793116314

There Were Times

True stories of Service experiences.
ISBN 9798649628792

Dearest Darling

A collection of his Wife's letters to himself during a period of Duty abroad, which highlights the daily problems and issues that service families have to deal with in the absence of the Father.
ISBN 9798629844174

All these books are available from Amazon Publishing

www.ingramcontent.com/pod-product-compliance
Lightning Source LLC
LaVergne TN
LVHW050551160826
845677LV00011B/2269

* 9 7 9 8 7 5 1 1 0 3 4 5 3 *